Might

is

Right

"*Must we then speak of this subject also; and shall we write concerning things that are not to be told, and shall we publish things not to be divulged, and secrets not to be spoken aloud?*"

—Julian the Emperor

"*The law immutable, indestructible, eternal; not like those of to-day and yesterday, but made ere time began.*"

—Sophocles

Might is Right

or

The Survival of the fittest

by

Ragnar Redbeard, LL.D.

(University of Chicago)

Loompanics Unlimited
Port Townsend, Washington

MIGHT IS RIGHT
Published by:
Loompanics Unlimited
PO Box 1197
Port Townsend, WA 98368
Printed in U.S.A.

Typesetting, layout and design by Patrick Michael

CONTENTS

INTRODUCTION

RAGNAR REDBEARD AND THE RIGHT OF MIGHT
by S.E. Parker

"It is surely one of the most incendiary works ever to be published anywhere."
—James J. Martin

"A vitriolic, racist hymn to the doctrine of force."
—Chris Cuneen

A MAN

Might Is Right is a book whose survival has nothing to do with popular acclaim or academic attention. It has, nonetheless, been read and discussed by a continuing circle of individuals for some 85 years, necessitating several editions. Originally published in 1896, it was reprinted as late as 1972. Erratic, inspiring, infuriating, a mixture of individualistic sense and collective nonsense, it outlines a case for "social darwinism" that is one of the frankest and most powerful I have ever seen.

There is no certainty as to who the author, Ragnar Redbeard, was. The most likely candidate is a man named Arthur Desmond who was red-bearded, red-haired and whose poetry was very similar to that written by Redbeard. Born in New Zealand of an Irish father and an English mother, his actual date of birth is unknown, 1842 and 1859 being two of the years given. While in New Zealand, Desmond stood as a radical candidate for parliament, organized trade unions, championed the ideas of Henry George, supported the Maori leader Te Kooti, and edited a radical paper called *The Tribune*.

i

In 1892 Desmond left New Zealand for Sydney, Australia. Here he continued his political activities, edited *Hard Cash* and *The Standard Bearer*, wrote poetry which influenced the famous Australian poet, Henry Lawson, joined the Labour Party, and associated with radical personalities like John Dwyer who had known Marx and Bakunin. It is said that he left Australia in 1895, taking with him the unpublished manuscript of *Might is Right.*

Any account of Desmond's subsequent career after leaving Australia is largely based on conjecture. He is said to have published *Redbeard's Review* in London, to have lived in Chicago, where he co-authored a book called *Rival Ceasars* with Will H. Dilg (using the pseudonym "Desmond Dilg" for the occasion), and edited the *Lion's Paw* under the name of Richard Thurland. His date of death is not certain. One version has him dying in Palestine in 1918 "while on service with General Allenby's troops," another version claims he died in 1926, again in Palestine. On the other hand, I have been told that he was running a bookshop in Chicago as late as 1927. And this is to discount not only the more bizarre stories such as that he was really Ambrose Bierce and was shot during the Mexican Revolution, but also the fact that there seems to be no definite evidence that Redbeard and Desmond were the same individual....

A BOOK

What is certain, however, is that if Desmond was Redbeard, then his views must have undergone a drastic change toward the end of his stay in Australia. *Might Is Right* is no manifesto of a political radical intent on the "emancipation of the workers." I cannot conceive of any of our contemporary saviours of the proletariat recommending it as required reading, even though it is claimed that it influenced some of the early Wobblies. And it certainly has no appeal for those sentimental totalitarians who profess "care" and "love" for mankind.

Redbeard sets out the theme of his book in a prefatory note entitled "All Else Is Error."

"The natural world is a world of war; the natural man is a warrior; the natural law is tooth and claw. All else is error. A condition of combat everywhere exists. We are born into perpetual conflict. It is our inheritance even as it was the inheritance of previous generations. The 'condition of combat' may be disguised with the holy phrases of St. Francis, or the soft, deceitful doctrines of a Kropotkin or a Tolstoy, but it cannot eventually be evaded by any human being...It rules all things...and it *decides* all who imagine policemanized populations, internationally regulated tranquility, and State organized industrialism so joyful, blessed and divine."

But in this war of each against all there are only a small number of victors. They alone conquer power and enjoy the loot. This is because "The great mass of men who inhabit the world of today have no initiative, no originality or independence of thought, but are mere subjective individualities, who never had the slightest voice in fashioning the ideas that they formally revere." The "average man...is a born thrall habituated from childhood to be governed by others." The majority of the common people can never become free, they "are but the sediment from which all the more valuable elements have long been distilled...Mastership is right, mastership is natural, mastership is eternal. But only for those who cannot overthrow it, and trample it beneath their hoofs."

On the other hand, the strong man is the free man and "freemen should never regulate their conduct by the suggestion or dicta of others, for when they do they are no longer free." The free man is "above all laws, all constitutions, all theories of right and wrong. He supports and defends them, of course, so long as they suit his own end, but if they don't then he annihilates them by the easiest and most direct method." "Liberty is honestly definable as a state of complete bodily and mental self-mastership...and thoroughgoing independence from all official coercion or restraint." It is synonymous with proprietorship. To be property-less and unarmed is the condition of actual dependence and servitude. Unarmed citizens are enslaved citizens, always. Liberty without property is a myth, a nursery tale, believable only by babbling babies.

Redbeard rejects equality as another myth. Let us take the notion of "equality before the law." "By what rational method can any two litigants be placed in a position of unconditioned 'equality before the law?' First of all, plaintiff and defendant always possess totally different physical and mental characteristics, different personal magnetisms—and different sized bank balances. Also all judges, juries and legal officials are unequal in temperament, ability, courage and honesty. Each one has his own peculiar idiosyncracies, prejudices, inferiorities, superstitions and—price. ...No two men are born alike: each one being literally born under his own particular star...'Equality before the law' is just a meaningless catchphrase."

Equality is a lie because "every atom of organic matter has its own vital peculiarity. Every animate being is different in osseous structure and chemical composition. Ethnology, biology, history, all proclaim equality to be a myth. Even the great epics of antiquity are all glorifications of inequality: inequality of the mind, inequality of birth, of courage or condition...Mentally and morally, every breathing being is a self-poised monad—a differentiated ego. No two germs, planets, suns, or stars are alike. Among the higher vertebrates this is especially so, and consequently the only law that men ought to honour or respect is the law that originates and finds its final sanction *in themselves*—in their own consciousness."

For Ragnar Redbeard, then, life is struggle, life is war and in this war those who are the strongest, and have set aside the authority of laws and moral codes as suitable only for the submissive mass, will be the winners. They will remain winners, however, only to the extent that they can continue to prove themselves the strongest. If others arise who are stronger than they, then they will lose and new masters will take their place. In this way the "survival of the fittest" will prevail and will no longer be hampered or denied by doctrines of brotherhood or equality which have no roots in reality.

Redbeard does not deny the existence of oppression and exploitation now or in his future world of the strong. What he does deny are the hypocritical claims of the power-seekers that they are doing what they do out of altruistic love for those they want to dominate. Legalism and moralism are the masks of connivers and their acceptance by the strong will lead to weakness and degeneration. Redbeard's position is not all that far from the Marquis de Sade, when he wrote: "Individuals who are not animated by strong passions are merely mediocre beings. It is only strong passions which can produce great men; when one is no longer...passionate, one becomes stupid. This point established, are not laws dangerous which inhibit the passions?"

A CRITIQUE

Although Redbeard claims to scorn moral codes, stating that "all arbitrary codes of right and wrong are insolent invasions of personal liberty" and that greatness lies "in being beyond and above all moral measurements," he is, nonetheless, a moralist. He makes plain his antagonism to Judeo-Christian morality, but his whole approach is shot through with the perennial moralistic desire to redeem the human race from "evil." For him, what is "natural" is "right" and the further human beings get away from "Nature," the further they depart from "right." Leaving aside the fact that "Nature" is a mental construct, not a fact, and that "Man" is nothing but an aggregate of individuals, the question remains

iv

as to how Redbeard would square his belief that "every breathing being" is "a differentiated ego" with his demand that all these differentiated egos accept the common goal of being "natural"—as he defines it. If I am unique, then what it is in my "nature" to be will not be the same as what it is in the "nature" of other individuals to be. Indeed, what is "natural" for me may well be "unnatural" for others, and a collision unavoidable. Redbeard's interpretation of "social darwinism" clearly allows for this, but his morality of "Nature" equally clearly negates it.

In fact, this contradiction is starkly illustrated by Redbeard himself when he comes to treat sexual relations between men and women. On the same page he proclaims that "moral principles...are artificial human enactments, but not necessarily natural, honest or true. Moral codes are the black terror of all dastards," and then goes on to state that "readers must distinctly understand that *sexual morality* is nowise condemned in these pages." This is because "women are frail beings at the best of times...they must be held in thorough subjection" for "woe unto the Race if ever these lovable creatures should break loose from mastership, and become the rulers or equals of Man." He follows this warning with a denunciation of "sexual degeneracy," "promiscuity," and other "evils," in a language redolent of the very Christian morality he so fiercely attacks elsewhere. "If our modern Sodoms," he writes, "were all razed to the ground, how Nature in all her perennial purity would rejoice exultantly!" Substitute "God" for "Nature" and what religious moralist would object?

Redbeard's view of the "nature" of women is in no way consistent. In one paragraph of his chapter on "Love, Women and War" he repeats his opinion of women as being "incapable of self-mastership...mere babies in worldly concerns," but in the next paragraph writes that "when their passions are stirred women have performed deeds of heroism (and terror) that even a man with nerves of steel would hesitate at...They have led armies and been criminals of the darkest dye." In claiming that women are destined to be "subjects" and at the same time are capable of being "rulers," Redbeard effectively destroys his own case for male superiority and, what is more, seems oblivious of the fact that he is doing it!

Redbeard is also a racist believing that Anglo-Saxons are the superior race. Blacks, Jews, Asiatics and "degenerate whites" are all excluded from his class of supermen. His racism, however, undermines the logic of his "philosophy of power." In a typical description of his philosophy he writes of the capitalist that he "can 'do as he likes with his own,' *as long as he has the power.* He may own the earth...if he wants to, and he may buy or sell men and nations if he feels inclined to or thinks it profitable. There is in Nature no limit to his energies or ambitions. All that is needed is power equal to his energies or ambitions. All that is needed is power equal to the design. But the same principles may be acted upon by any other man or association of men, and in the conflict that ensues *fitness is proved—absolutely and without doubt.* The 'rights of the rich' are what they *can* maintain and the 'rights of the poor' are not less. No bounds are set to the accumulation of property, and none whatever to its re-distribution."

If, therefore, "all that is needed" for the survival of the fittest is "power equal to the design" and "the same principles may be acted upon by any other man or association of men," this must logically apply to all human beings. It follows that if a Black, a Jew, an Asiatic or a "degenerate white," proves to be stronger than one of Redbeard's Anglo-Saxon supermen, then he has no grounds upon which he can deny the victor his spoils. If I can do as I like with my own as long as I have the power, then it does not matter what race or colour I am for I have shown that I am the powerful one. Redbeard's racism, like his sexism, is therefore completely inconsistent with his own "philosophy of power" since he can only defend it by using collectivist notions that deny his individualist premise that there are no "rights" outside the "might" of the individual.

Might Is Right is a work flawed by major contradictions. Like the Christian bible it can be used as a source for the most incompatible views, but unlike that venerable collection of idiocies and myths it is sustained by a crude vigor that at its most coherent can help to clear away not a few of the religious, moral and political superstitions bequeathed to us by our ancestors. Whoever Ragnar Redbeard was, and whatever criticisms may be justly levelled at his book, he remains worthy of the attention of all who are conscious that their "rights" are equal to their power.

For supplying information and speculations, the author would like to thank Chris Cuneen of the Australian Dictionary of Biography, Bob James, historian of Australian Anarchism, and Edward C. Weber, head of the Labadie Collection, University of Michigan. Thanks are also due to former Chicago soapboxers Slim Brundage and the late Dave Tullman for their memories.

S.E. Parker edits and publishes the anarchist individualist review **Ego**, and wrote the introduction to the Rebel Press edition of Max Stirner's **The Ego and His Own**. The above essay originally appeared in issue #13 (Winter, 1982-83) of **The Storm!**, 227 Columbus Avenue #2E, New York, NY 10023.

OPPORTUNITIES

A man's opportunities are never exhausted so long as other men (who are not his friends) possess millions of acres and thousands of tons of gold.

The guarded treasure halls and iron-clad temples of modern kings and presidents; high priests and millionaires, are positively the richest the world has ever known.

Bulging are they with the vast hoards of silver and diamonds and gold.

Here, then, is opportunity on a colossal scale. Here is the goal of the Ceasers, Nebuchadnezzars and Napoleons in the days that are coming.

All is ready and prepared for them, even as in olden times.

Ceasar carried off the treasures of Egypt, Greece, Gaul and Rome.

Napoleon looted the money vaults of Venice, Vienna, Madrid, Berlin and Moscow. London only escaped him.

Nebuchadnezzar plundered the Temple of Zion, where the Jews kept all their deposits and drank his beer and wine out of Jehovah's pots of gold.

Napoleon, Ceasar, Nebuchadnezzar! There were three great men, were they not? And in this their greatness consisted—they seized their opportunities.

1

Behold the crucifix, what does it symbolize? Pallid incompetence hanging on a tree.

Lo, I hear the fighters coming
Over hill and dale and plain.
With the battle cry of ages
In a Rebel world again.

Who'd forge their swords to plow-shares,
Shall sweat in bitter yokes,
The free-born race and fearless
Must deal out battle strokes.

In the wars of the Great Ceasar, and Grim Hannibal, in the times of Belzchazzar, the Pharaohs and all; the days of Rienzi and Roland the Bold; all banners were waving for WOMEN and GOLD.

It is might against might, remember, by land and sea, man against man, money against money, brains against brains, and—everything to the winner.

ALL ELSE IS ERROR

The natural world is a world of war; the natural man is a warrior; the natural law is tooth and claw. All else is error. A condition of combat everywhere exists. We are born into perpetual conflict. It is our inheritance even as it was our heritage of previous generations. This "condition of combat" may be disguised with the holy phrases of St. Francis, or the soft deceitful doctrines of a Kropotkin or Tolstoi, but it cannot be eventually evaded by any human being or any tribe of human beings. It is *there* and it stays *there*, and each man (whether he will or not) has to reckon with it. It rules all things; it governs all things; it reigns over all things and it *decides* all who imagine policemanized populations, internationally regulated tranquility, and State organized industrialism so joyful blessed and divine.

THE VICTOR GETS THE GOLD

Virtue is rewarded in *this* world remember. Natural law makes no false judgments. Its decisions are true and just even when dreadful. The victor gets the gold and the land every time. He also gets the fairest maidens, the glory tributes. And—why should it be otherwise? Why should the delights of life go to failures and cowards? Why should the spoils of battle belong to the unwarlike? That would be insanity, utterly unnatural and immoral.

3

1

INTRODUCTORY

In this arid wilderness of steel and stone I raise up my voice that you may hear.

To the East and to the West I beckon. To the North and to the South I show a sign—

Proclaiming "Death to the weakling, wealth to the strong."

Open your eyes that you may hear, O! men of mildewed minds and listen to me ye laborious millions!

For I stand forth to challenge the wisdom of the world; to interrogate the "laws" of man and of "God."

I request reasons for your Golden Rule and ask the why and wherefore of your Ten Commands.

Before none of your printed idols do I bend in acquiescence and he who saith "thou shalt" to me is my mortal foe.

I demand proof over all things, and accept (with reservations) even that which is true.

I dip my forefinger in the watery blood of your impotent mad-redeemer (your Divine Democrat—your Hebrew Madman) and write over his thorn-torn brow "The true prince of Evil—the king of the Slaves!"

No hoary falsehood shall be a truth to me—no cult or dogma shall encramp my pen.

I break away from all conventions. Alone, untrammelled. I raise up in stern invasion of the standard of Strong.

I gaze into the glassy eye of your fearsome Jehovah, and pluck him by the beard—I uplift a broad-axe and split open his worm-eaten skull.

I blast out the ghastly contents of philosophic whited sepulchres and laugh with sardonic wrath.

Then reaching up the festering and varnished facades of your haughtiest moral dogmas, I write thereon in letters of blazing scorn:—"Lo and behold, all this is fraud!"

I deny all things! I question all things!

And yet! And yet!

—Gather around me O! ye death-defiant and the earth itself shall be thine, to have and to hold.

What is your "civilization and progress" if its only outcome is hysteria and downgoing?

What is "government and law" if their ripened harvests are men without sap?

What are "religious and literatures" if their grandest productions are hordes of faithful slaves?

What is "evolution and culture" if their noxious blossoms are sterilized women?

What is education and enlightenment if their dead-sea-fruit is a caitiff race, with rottenness in its bones?

2

How is it that "men of light and leading" hardly ever call in question the manufactured "moral codes," under which our once vigorous Northern race is slowly and surely eating out its heart in peaceful inaction and laborious dry-rot?

Standard "moral principles" are arbitrarily assumed by their orthodox apologists to be a fixed and unalterable quantity, and that to doubt the devine-rightness of these "principles" is treason and sacrilege. When the greatest thinkers of a race are incapable, or afraid to perform their manifest logical function, it is scarcely to be wondered that average citizens are also somewhat unwilling to "risk life, fortune and sacred honor" for the overthrow of popularized "right and wrong" concepts, that they know from bitter personal experience are unworkable falsities. Although the average man feels in his heart that nearly all political and religious conventionalisms are dynamic deceits, yet how cautiously he avoids any open display of antagonism thereto? He has not the courage of his opinions. He is afraid to say openly what he thinks secretly. In other words he is living in a state of subjectiveness; of vassalage. He allows his brain to be dominated and held in bondage by the brain of another. From his infancy he has been deliberately subjected to a continuous external pressure, especially designed to coerce his understanding into strict accord with pre-arranged views of moral, political or religious "duty." He has not been permitted one moment of real mental liberty. He imbibed fraudulent conventionalisms with his mother's milk. He listens to the most hideous lies being glorified in his presence as

6

sublime truths. He hears falsehoods sung in swelling chorus. He hears them sounded on bugles of silver and brass. He hears them intoned by "congregations of the faithful" amid peals of sacred music, and the solemn roll of chanted prayer. Thus his mind is sterilized by authority before it has had a chance to mature. Thus youth is mentally castrated, that its natural vitality may be afterwards used up in the yoke of custom—which is the yoke of slavery. In the nursery, at school, and at college, plastic brain-pulp is deliberately forced into the pre-arranged mold. Everything that a corrupt civilization can do, is done to compress the growing intellect into unnatural channels. Thus the great mass of men who inhabit the world today have no initiative, no originality or independence of thought, but are mere subjective individualities, who have never had the slightest voice in fashioning the ideals that they formally revere.

Although the average man has taken no part in manufacturing moral codes and statute laws, yet how he obeys them with dog-like submissiveness! He is trained to obedience, like oxen are broken to the yoke of their masters. He is a born thrall habituated from childhood to be governed by others.

Chinese civilization deliberately distorts its children's feet, by swathing them in bandages of silk and hoop iron. Christian civilization crushes and cramps the minds of its youth by means of false philosophies, artificial moral codes and ironclad political creeds. Deleterious sub-theories of good and evil are systematically injected into our natural literatures, and gradually (without serious obstruction) they crystallize themselves into cast-iron formulas, infallible constitutions, will-o-the-wisp evangels, and other deadly epidemics.

Modern "leaders of thought" are almost wholly wanting in originality and courage. Their wisdom is foolishness, their remedies poison. They idiotically claim that they guide the destinies of nations, whereas, in reality, they are but the flotsam and scum-froth that glides smoothly down the dark stream of decadence.

"Thus all the people of the earth are helpless,
Seeing those that lead are blind."

Mankind is aweary, aweary of its sham prophets; its demagogues and its statesmen. It crieth out for kings and heroes. It demands a nobility—a nobility that cannot be hired with money, like slaves or beasts of burden. The world awaits the coming of mighty men of valor, great destroyers; destroyers of all that is vile, angels of death. We are sick unto nausea of the "good Lord Jesus," terror-stricken under the executive of priest, mob and proconsul. We are tired to death of "Equality." Gods are at a discount, devils are in demand. He who would rule the coming age, must be hard, cruel, and deliberately intrepid, for softness assails not successfully the idols of the multitude. Those idols must be smashed into fragments, burnt into ashes, and that cannot be done by the gospel of love.

The living forces of evil are to be found in the living ideals of today.

The Commandments and laws and moral codes that we are called upon to reverence and obey are themselves insidious enginery of decadence. It is moral principles that manufacture beggars. It is golden rules that glorify meekness. It is statute laws that make spaniels of men.

A man may keep every one of the Ten Commandments and yet remain a fool all the days of his life. He may obey every written law of the land, and yet be a caitiff and a slave. He may "love Jesus," delight in the golden rule and yet continue to the hour of his death, a failure and dependent. Truly the way to hell is by fulfilling the commandments of God. If the all-conquering race to which we belong is not to irretrievably dwindle into multitudinous nothingness (like the inferior herds it has outdistanced or enslaved), then it is essential that the Semitic spider webs (so astutely woven for ages into the brains of our chiefs) be remorselessly torn out by the very roots, even though the tearing out process be both painful and bloody.

If we would retain and defend our inherited manhood, we must not permit ourselves to be forever rocked to repose with the sweet lullabies of eastern idealisms. Too long we have been hypnotized by the occult charm of Hebrew Utopianism. If we continue to obey the insidious spell that has been laid upon us, we will wake up some dread morning with the gates of hell—"of hell upon earth"—yawning wide open, to close again upon us forever.

The idea of hell is in some respects a truthful conception, suggestive of actual fact. If we terrestialize the location, there is nothing inharmonious about it. Many a race, many a tribe, and many a mighty empire has gone down into a grimly realistic sheol. Is it not right and just, that the vile, the base and the degenerate (that is to say the slave nations of the earth) should be punished pitilessly for their creeping cowardice? Is it not right that they should be, as it were, fried and toasted—should swim in pools of boiling blood, or dance sweltering satanic glees, with blistered feet and straining eyeballs on red-hot Saharas of gravel and sand?

In actual operation Nature is cruel and merciless to men, as to all other beings. Let a tribe of human animals live a rational life, Nature will smile upon them and their posterity; but let them attempt to organize an unnatural mode of existence, an equality elysium, and they will be punished even to the point of extermination.

 3

All ethics, politics and philosophies are pure assumptions, built upon assumptions. They rest on no sure basis. They are but shadowy castles-in-the-air erected by day-dreamers, or by rogues, upon nursery fables. It is time they were firmly planted upon an enduring foundation. This can never be accomplished until the racial mind has first been thoroughly cleansed and drastically disinfected of its depraved, alien, and demoralizing concepts of right and wrong. In no human brain can sufficient space be found for the relentless logic of hard fact, until all pre-existent delusions have been finally annihilated. Half-measures are of no avail, we must go down to the very roots and tear them out, even to the last fibre. We must be, like nature, hard, cruel, relentless.

Too long the dead hand has been permitted to sterilize living thought -- too long, right and wrong, good and evil, have been inverted by false prophets. In the days that are at hand, neither creed nor code must be accepted upon authority, human, superhuman or 'divine.' (Morality and conventionalism are for subordinates.) Religions and constitutions and all arbitrary principles, every mortal theorem, must be deliberately put to the question. No moral dogma must be taken for granted -- no standard of measurement deified. There is nothing inherently sacred about moral codes. Like the wooden idols of long ago, they are all the work of human hands, and what man has made, man can destroy.

He that is slow to believe anything and everything is of great understanding, for belief in one false principle is the beginning of all unwisdom. The chief duty of every new age is to up-raise new men to determine its liberties, to lead toward its material success -- to rend (as it were) the rusty padlocks and chains of dead custom that always prevent healthy expansion. Theories and ideals and constitutions, that may have meant life and hope and freedom for our ancestors, may now mean destruction, slavery and dishonor to us. As environments change no human ideal standeth sure.

Wherever, therefore, a lie has built unto itself a throne, let it be assailed without pity and without regret, for under the dominance of a falsehood, no nation can permanently prosper. Let established sophisms be dethroned, rooted out, burnt and destroyed, for they are a standing menace to all true nobility of thought and action. Whatever alleged "truth" is proven by results, to be but an empty fiction, let it be unceremoniously flung into the outer darkness, among the dead gods, dead empires, dead philosophies, and other useless lumber and wreckage.

The most dangerous of all enthroned lies is the holy, the sanctified, the privileged lie -- the lie that "everybody" believes to be a model truth. It is the fruitful mother of all other popular errors and delusions. It is hydra-headed. It has a thousand roots. It is a social cancer. The lie that is known to be a lie is half eradicated, but the lie that even intelligent persons regard as a sacred fact -- the lie that has been inculcated around a mother's knee -- is more dangerous to contend against than a creeping pestilence. Popular lies have ever been the most potent enemies of personal liberty. There is only one way to deal with them. Cut them out, to the very core, just as cancers are. Exterminate them root and branch, or they will surely eat us all up. We must annihilate them, or they will us. Half and half remedies are of no avail.

However, when a lie has gone too far -- when it has taken up its abode in the very tissues, bones and brains of a people, then all remedies are useless. Even the lancet is of no avail. Repentance of past misdeeds cannot "save" decadents from extermination. The fatal bolt is shot; and into the fiery furnace of wholesale slavery, and oblivion, they must go, to be there righteously consumed. From their ashes something new, something nobler, may possibly evolve, but even that is the merest optimistic supposition.

In nature the wages of sin is *always* death. Nature does not love the wrong-doer, but endeavors in every possible way to destroy him. Her curse is on the brow of the "meek and lowly." Her blessing is on the very hearts' blood of the strong and the brave. Only Jews and Christs and other degenerates, think that rejuvenation can ever come through law and prayer. "All the tears of all the martyrs" might just as well have never been shed.

 4

Whatsoever a people believeth shall make it free, enslave it, or corrode its very marrow in strict accordance with natural order. Consequently if a people place implicit faith in what philosophers teach them, they are liable to be duped. If many nations are so duped, their deception is a menace to the liberty of the world.

Freemen should never regulate their conduct by the suggestions or dicta of others, for when they do so, they are no longer free. No man ought to obey any contract, written or implied, except he himself has given his personal and formal adherence thereto, when in a state of mental maturity and unrestrained liberty. It is only slaves that are born into contracts, signed and sealed by their progenitors. The freeman is born free, lives free, and dies free. He is (even though living in an artificial civilization) above all laws, all constitutions, all theories of right and wrong. He supports and defends them of course, as long as they suit his own end, but if they don't, then he annihilates them by the easiest and most direct method.

There is no obligation upon any man to passive obedience, when his life, his liberty and his property are threatened by footpad, assassin or statesmen.

One of Columbus's lieutenants in the West Indies captured a Carib chief by means of a subtle strategem. The chief was invited to a feast and when there, persuaded with honeyed words to don (on horseback) a set of brightly polished steel manacles; it being cunningly represented to him that the irons were the regalia of sovereignty. He foolishly believed his astute flatterer, and when the chains were firmly clasped around his limbs, he was led away, to die of vermin, turning a mill in a Spanish dungeon. What those glittering manacles were to the Indian chieftain, constitutions, laws, moral codes, and Hebrew dominated civilizations, are to the nations of the earth. Indeed, under the name of Progress and Social Evolution, mankind has been lured into fetid dungeons, where it labors unceasingly and for naught, in darkness, despair and shame. Like that Spanish lieutenant the masters of the earth first flatter their dupes, in order to more easily enchain them. Who talks nowadays of the "sovereign people," without a laugh of derision? And yet it was once thought to be a term full of significance. Their 'sovereignty' is now acknowledged sham, and their freedom a dream. The sovereign people be—.

It is clear, therefore, that the man or nation that would retain liberty, or be really safe, must accept no formula as final—must trust in nothing written or unwritten, living or dead—must believe neither in special Jehovahs, nor weeping Saviours— neither in raging devils, nor in devilish philosophies—neither in ghosts, nor in idols, nor in laws—nor in women, nor in man.

"O threats of hell, and hopes of paradise,
One thing at least is certain—this life flies;
One thing is certain and all the rest is—lies,
The flower that once has bloomed forever dies."

❧ 5 ❧

He who saith unto himself, "I must believe, I must not question" is not a man but a mere pusilanimous mental gelding. He who believes "because it has been handed down"is a menial in his heart; and he who believes "because it has been written" is a fool in his folly. Sagacious spirits doubt all things, and hold fast only to that which is demonstrably true.

The rules of life are not to be found in Korans, Bibles, Decalogues and Constitutions, but rather the rules of decadence and death. The "law of laws" is not written in Hebrew consonants or upon tables of brass and stone, but in every man's own heart. He who obeys any standard of right and wrong, but the one set up by his own conscience, betrays himself into the hands of his enemies, who are ever laying in wait to bind him to their millstones. And generally a man's most dangerous enemies are his neighbors.

Masterful men laugh with contempt at spiritual thunders, and have no occasion to dread the decisions of any human tribunal. They are above and beyond all that. Laws and regulations are only for conquered vassals. The free man does not require them. He may manufacture and post up Decalogue regulations, to bind and control dependents with, but he does not himself bow down before those inventions of his own hands—except as a lure.

State books and golden rules, were made to fetter slaves and fools. Very useful are they, for controlling the herds of sentenced convicts, who fill the factories, and cultivate the fields. All moral principles, therefore, are the servitors, not the masters of the strong. Power made moral codes, and Power abrogates them.

A *man* is under no obligation to obey anything or anybody. It is only serving-men that must obey, because they are caitiffs by birth, breeding, and condition. Morals are only required in an immoral community, that is to say a community held in a state of conquest.

Fear God, bridle the spirit and obey the law, is advice most excellent, as from a philosopher to a yokel, but when directed in all earnestness at a *man* of inherent might, he smiles to himself in silent scorn. Full well he knows that in actual life the path to victory and renown, does not lie through Gethsemanies, but over fallen enemies, the ruins of rival combines, through Aceldamas. "Meekness of spirit" is regarded by him as a convenient superstition, very useful for regulating the lives of his servants, his women and his children, but otherwise inoperative.

12

"I rest my hopes on nothing" proclaimed Goethe, and masterful minds in all ages have never done otherwise. This unspoken thought gives to all truly great men their manifest superiority over the brainless, vociferating herd. The "common people" have always had to be fooled with some written or wooden or golden Idol—some constitution, declaration or gospel. Consequently the majority of them have ever been mental thralls, living and dying in an atmosphere of strong illusion. They are befooled and hypnotized even to this hour, and a large portion of them must remain so, until time is no more. Indeed the masses of mankind are but the sediment from which all the more valuable elements have long ago been distilled. They are totally incapable of real freedom, and if it was granted to them, they would straightaway vote themselves a master, or a thousand masters within twenty-four hours. Mastership is right—Mastership is natural—Mastership is eternal. But only for those who cannot overthrow it, and trample it beneath their hoofs. Is it not a fact that in actual life, the ballot-box votes of ten million subjective personalities are as thistle down in the balance, when weighed against the far seeing thought, and material prowess of, say, ten strong silent men?

🐾 6 🐾

It is notorious, universally so, that the blackest falsehoods are ever decked out in the most brilliant and gorgeous regalia. Clearly, therefore, it is the brave man's duty to regard all sacred things, all legal things, all constitutional things, all holy things, with more than usual suspicion. "I deny, and I affirm," is the countersign of material freedom. "I believe, and I obey," is the shibboleth of serfage. Belief is a flunky, a feminine—Doubt is a creator, a master. He who denies fundamentals is in triple armor clad. Indeed he is invulnerable. On the other hand, it has been said that every belief, every philosophy, has some truth in it, but so we might add has every insanity.

Strong men are not deterred from pursuing their aim by anything. They go straight to the goal, and that goal is Beauty, Wealth and Material Power. The mission of Power is to control and exploit the powerless, for to be powerless is to be a criminal. The world would indeed be a house of horrors, if all men were "good" and all women—padlocked.

As far as human searchlights have yet penetrated, into the darkness that enshrouds the origin of nations, we see the subduers and the subdued, the plebians and the patricians, the chiefs who governed, and the vassals who obeyed. And there is nothing in the most modern social developments (of these deedless days) to warrant any belief that this ancient and natural division of human animals, into castes of superiors and inferiors, sovereigns and serfs, can ever be dispensed with. The slave-owner's whip cracked from the beginning and it will crack till the day of doom. In every kingdom, republic and empire on earth, we have (in one disguise or another) the master and the slave—the ruler and the ruled. In the course of centuries, names alone have changed, essentials have remained the same. Forms of royalty may alter but kings can never die. There was mastership at the beginning, and there will be mastership to the end. We build, but as our fathers built. Change is not progress, nor numbers advance.

Every one who would be free must show his power. Unalterable remains the basis of all earthly greatness. He who exalteth himself shal be exalted, and he who humbleth himself shal be righteously trodden beneath the hoofs of the herd. "The humble" are only fit for dog's meat. Bravery includes every virtue—humility, every crime. He who is afraid to risk his life must never be permitted to win anything.

Human rights and wrongs are not determined by Justice, but by Might. Disguise it as you may, the naked sword is still king-maker and king-breaker, as of yore. All other theories are lies and—lures.

Therefore! If you would conquer wealth and honor, power and fame you must be practical, grim, cool and merciless. You must ride to success (by preference) over the necks of your foemen. Their defeat is your strength. Their downfall is your uplifting. Only the powerful can be free, and Power is non-moral. Life is real, life is earnest, and neither heaven nor hell its final goal. And love, and joy, and birth, and death, and fate, and strife, shall be forever.

This earth is a vast whirl of warring atoms—a veritable revolving cock-pit. Each molecule, each animal, fights for its life. You must fight for yours, or surrender. Look well into it, therefore, that your breaks and spurs, your fangs and claws, are as sharp as steel, and as effective as science can make them.

Though, the survival of the strongest is the logic of events, yet personal cowardice is the great vice of our demoralized age. Cowardice is corroding the brain and blood of our race, but men have learnt to disguise this terrible infirmity, behind the canting whine of "humanity" and "goodness." Words flow instead of blood, and terrible insults are exchanged, instead of terrible blows.

How rich this degenerate world is in small, petty-souled, good-for-nothings, who are forever excusing their infantile ineptitude behind some plausible phrase—some conventional make-believe?

14

Courage, I say! Courage, not goodness, is the great desideratum—courage, that requires neither tin horns, nor calcium lights, nor brass bands, nor shouting multitudes to call it into effective action.

But courage that goes its way *alone*, as undauntedly as when it marches to 'victory or death' amid the menacing stride of armed and bannered legions.

Courage, that delights in danger—Courage, that knows not despair! Courage that proudly, defiantly, smiles on death!

Courage, that regards with equal loathing the multitude's mad howls of hate, its stupid hee-haws and its stridulating 'tremendous applause'.

Courage, that asks no quarter, even with the knife at its throat—courage that is stiff-necked, unyielding, sullen, pitiless!

Courage, that never falters—never retreats!

Courage, that looks down with supreme disdain upon all slave regulations, upon all rights and wrongs, upon all good and evil!

Courage, that has made up its mind to conquer or—perish!

That is the kind of courage this world lacks. That is the kind of courage that aids by active co-operation the survival of the Fittest—the survival of the Best.

That is the kind of courage that has never turned a master's mill.

That is the kind of courage that never will turn it.

That is the kind of courage that will die, rather than turn it.

"When Svipdag came to the enclosure, the gate of the burg was shut (for it was customary to ask leave to come in and see, or take part in the war games). Svipdag did not take that trouble, but broke open the gate and rode into the yard."

"Queen Yisa said: 'this man will be welcome here.'"*

---

* Ancient Norse Saga.

2

ICONOCLASTIC

As far as Sociology is concerned, we must either abandon our reason, or abandon Christ.

He is pre-eminently the pophet of unreason—the preacher of the rabble-rabies. All that is enervating and destructive of manhood, he glorifies—all that is self-reliant and heroic, he denounces. Lazarus the filthy and diseased vagrant, is his hero of heros; and Dives the sane, energetic citizen is his 'awful' example of baseness and criminality. He praises "the humble" and he curses the proud. He blesses the failures, and damns the successful. All that is noble, he perverts—all that is atrocious he upholds. He inverts all the natural instincts of mankind, and urges us to live artificial lives. He commands the demonization of virtues that aggrandise a people, and advises his admirers to submit in quietness to every insult, contumely, indignity; to be slaves, de-facto. Indeed there is scarce one thought in the whole of his Dicta that is practically true.

O, Christ! O, Christ! Thou artful fiend! Thou Great Subverter!— What an amazing Eblis-glamour, thou hast cast over the world? Thou mean insignificant-minded Jew!

Why is it that our modern philosophers are so mortally afraid to boldly challenge the 'inspired' utopianism of this poor self-deluded Gallilean mountaineer—this preacher of all eunuch-virtues—of self-abasement, of passive suffering?

The sickly humanitarian ethics, so eloquently rayed forth by Jesus Christ and his superstitious successors, in ancient Judea, and throughout the moribund Roman empire, are generally accepted in Anglo-Saxondom as the very elixir of immortal wisdom, the purest, wisest, grandest, most incontrovertible of all 'divine revelations,' or occult thaumaturgies. And yet when closely examined, they are found to be neither divine, occult, reasonable, nor even honest; but composed, almost exclusively, of the stuff that nightmares are made of; together with a strong dash of oriental legerdemain.

Through a thousand different channels, current politico-economic belief is dominated by the base communistic caballa of the 'man of many sorrows'; yet as a practical theorem, it is hardly ever critically examined. Why is it that the suggested social solutions promulgated by Jesus, Peter, Paul, James, and other Asiatic cataleptics, are accepted so meekly by us, upon trust? If these men were anything, they were crude socialist reformers with mis-shapen souls, preachers of a 'new heaven, and a new earth,' that is to say, demagogues—politicians-of-the-slums; and out of the slums, nothing that is noble can ever be born.

As agitators, Jesus and his modern continuators, shall be exclusively considered in these pages. However it must be distinctly understood, that the spiritual and temporal in all cosmogonies, are so intricately interwoven, that it is almost impossible to completely divorce them. Like the Siamese twins, Gods and Governments are inextricably bound together; so much so indeed, that if you kill one, the other cannot live. Hence the open or secret alliance, that has always existed between the politician and the priest.

Whatever their primitive purity (or impurity), all operative creedal philosophies are essentially civil and military codes, police regulations. "Religion is a power, a political engine, and if there was no God, I would have to invent one," said the great Napoleon. In letter and spirit, Christianity is above all things a political theory, and a theory that often takes the form of raging hysterics.

Religions are the matrix in which public institutions are generally molded. This has ever been well understood by the dominant leaders of mankind, from Numa to Brigham Young, from Solon to Loyola, from Constantine to the lowest Levite hireling, who gets paid in dimes and cents for his unctious mock—dithyrambs.

🦅 2 🦅

"All ye are brethren."

Are all men really bretheren?—Negro and Indian, Blackfellow, Kalmuck, and Coolie—the well-born, and the base-bred*—beer-soaked loafer, and hero-hearted patriot—belted chieftain and ignoble mechanic-slave—pot of iron and pot of clay?

What proof is there that the brotherhood-of-man hypothesis is in accordance with nature? On what trustworthy biologic, historic or other evidence does it rest? If it is natural, then rivalry,

---

* These terms are used in the strict Darwinian sense.

17

competition, and strife are unnatural. (And it is proposed to prove in this book, that strife, competition, rivalry, and the wholesale destruction of feeble types of men is not only natural, but highly necessary.) Has 'brotherhood' ever been tried upon earth? Where, when and with what final result? Is not self-assertion nobler, grander and more truly heroic than self-denial? Is not self-abasement but another term for voluntary vassalage; voluntary burden-bearing?

Christ might well and truthfully have said unto his followers "Come unto me all ye that are weary and heavy laden and I will bind you in unbreakable bonds, and load you down like an ass between two burdens."

The 'poor and ignorant' were his first followers—the vagrants, the disinherited shiftless classes; and to this very day, the poorer and more ignorant men and women are, the more eager are they to follow his religious ideals, or the political millenialisms that are distilled out of his delusions.

"If we only lived as Christ lived, what a beautiful world this would be," saith all thoughtless ones. If we lived as Christ lived, there would be none of us left to live. He begat no children; he labored not for his bread; he possessed neither house nor home: he merely talked. Consequently he must have existed on charity, or have stolen bread. 'If we all lived like Christ' would there have been anyone left to labor, to be begged from, to be stolen from? 'If we all lived like Christ' is thus a self-evident absurdity.

No wonder that it is recorded: "Not many wise after the flesh, not many mighty, not many noble are called; but God chose the foolish things of the world...and God chose the weak things of the world, and the things that are despised." Nothing else would have anything to do with him. Christ was indeed the prophet of the credulous rabble during three years of active agitation, and it abandoned him in his hour of need (what always happens under similar circumstances), for the rabble is ever cowardly, ungenerous, suspicious, unfathomably base. It has never yet had a leader of commanding ability (either in peace or in war), that it did not ultimately desert or betray, i.e., if he did not take the precaution to make himself its master.

After permitting Christ to be butchered, the mob thereupon set him up as their Divinity, and erected altars to his renown. Slaves, women, madmen, lepers, magdalenes, were the earliest Christians, and to this hour, women, children, slaves and lunatics are the raw material of the Christian Church.

Primitive Christianity cunningly appealed to the imagination of a world of superstitious slaves. (Eager for some mode of escape that meant not the giving and receiving of battle-strokes.) It

18

organized them for the overthrow of Heroic Principles; and substituted, for a genuine nobility based on battle-selection, a crafty theocracy founded upon priest-craft, hell-craft, alms-giving, politicalisms, and all that is impure and subterranean. It is a doctrine at once disgraceful in its antecedents, its teachers, and in itself. Truly has it been called 'the fatal dower of Constantine,' for it has suffocated, or is suffocating, the seeds of Heroism.

Both ancient and modern Christianism and all that has its root therein, is the negation of everything grand, noble, generous, heroic, and the glorification of everything feeble, atrocious, dishonorable, dastardly. The cross is now, and ever has been, an escutcheon of shame. It represents a gallows, and a Semite slave swinging thereon. For two thousand years it has absolutely overturned human reason; overthrown common sense, infected the world with madness, submissiveness, degeneracy.

Truly, there is a way which seemeth right unto a people, but the ends thereof are the ways of death.

Sound the loud timbrel,
O'er lands and o'er waves;
The Israelite triumphs!
The nations are—graves!

 3

Is the Golden Rule a rational rule—Is it not rather a menial rule—a coward rule—a best-policy rule? Why is it 'right' for one man to do unto others as he would have others do unto him and, what is right? If 'others' are unable to injure him or 'do good' to him, why should he consider them at all? Why should he take any more notice of them than of so many worms? If they are endeavoring to injure him, and able to do it, why should he refrain from returning the compliment? Should he not combat them, does not that give them carte-blanche to injure and destroy him? May it not be 'doing good' to others, to war against them, to annihilate them? May it not also be 'good' for them to war against others? (Again, what is 'good'?)

Is it reasonable to ask preying animals to do unto others as they would be done by—If they acted accordingly would they, could they, survive? If some only accepted the Golden Rule as their moral maxim, would they not become a prey to those who refused to abide thereby?

Upon what reasonable and abiding sanction does the 'Rule' rest—Has it ever been in actual operation among men—Can it ever be successfully practiced on earth—or anywhere else—Did

Jesus Christ practice it himself upon all occasions—Did His apostles, his 'sons of thunder' practice it—Did Peter the boaster do so, when he 'denied Him' for fear of arrest at the camp-fire—Did Judas the financier, when he sold him for net cash? Also how many of his modern lip-servants actually practice it in their daily business intercourse with each other. How many?

These questions require no formal answering. They answer themselves in the asking. And here it must be remembered that the best test of a witness is cross-examination.

'Do unto others as you would have others do to you,'
No baser precept ever fell from the lips of a feeble Jew.

It is from alleged moralisms of this sort, and fabulous 'principles' that our mob orators, our communards, revivalists, anarchists, red-republicans, democrats, and other mob-worshippers in general derive the infernal inspiration that they are perpetually hissing forth. Even the subversive pyrotechnic watchwords of their mephisto-millenium are to be found in the 'holy gospels.' Is it not written, "and God sendeth angels to destroy the people?"—Behold! these men are the 'angels' that He sends: politicians and reformers!

 4

'Love one another' you say is the supreme law, but what power has made it so—Upon what rational authority does the Gospel of Love rest—Is it even possible of practice, and what would result from its universal application to active affairs? Why should I not hate mine enemies, and hunt them down like the wild beasts they are? Again I ask, why? If I 'love' them does that not place me at their mercy? Is it natural for enemies to 'do good' unto each other and, what is 'good'? Can the torn and bloody victim 'love' the blood-splashed jaws that rend it limb from limb? Are we not all predatory animals by instinct? If humans ceased wholly from preying upon each other, could they continue to exist?

'Love your enemies and do good to them that hate you and despitefully use you,' is the despicable philosophy of the spaniel that rolls upon its back, when kicked. Obey it, O! reader, and you and all your posterity to the tenth generation shall be irretrievably and literally damned. They shall be hewers of wood, and carriers of water, degenerates, Gibeonites. But hate your enemies with a whole heart, and if a man smite you on one cheek, smash him down; smite him hip and thigh for self-preservation is the highest law.

20

He who turns the 'other cheek' is a cowardly dog—a Christian dog.

Give him blow for blow, scorn for scorn, doom for doom; with compound interest liberally added thereunto. Eye for eye, tooth for tooth, aye four-fold, a hundred-fold. Make yourself a Terror to your adversary and when he goeth his way, he will possess much additional wisdom to ruminate over. Thus shall you make yourself respected in all the walks of life, and your spirit—your *immortal* spirit—shall live, not in an intangible paradise, but in the brains and thews of your aggressive and unconquerable sons. After all, the true proof of manhood is a splendid progeny; and it is a scientific axiom that the timid animal transmits timidity to its descendants.

If men lived 'like brothers' and had no powerful enemies (neighbors) to contend with and surpass, they would rapidly lose all their best qualities; like certain oceanic birds that lose the use of their wings, because they do not have to fly from pursuing beasts of prey. If all men had treated each other with brotherly love since the beginning, what would have been the result now? If there had been no wars, no rivalry, no competition, no kingship, no slavery, no survival of the Toughest, no racial extermination; truly what a festering 'hell fenced in' this old globe would be?

 5

Reverend Ferdinand M. Sprague, of Chicago (who may be taken as a common specimen of the priest-politician), in a little pamphlet lately published, entitled "The Laws of Social Evolution" writes thus: "The sheet anchor of Socialism according to its ablest exponents, is the Holy Christian religion. Its motto founded on the precept 'Love they neighbor as thyself' is—'each for all, and all for each.' Its working principle for the present is altruism."*

Nearly all the canonized 'Fathers' of the early Roman propaganda (most of whom, by the way, were slaves, freedmen or eunuchs), advocated similar Ideals. Even now, the anointed and sanctified head of the Catholic Church resurrects the same hoary old utopianism, in a Jesuitic encyclical addressed to his flock. (How suggestive of being shorn and skinned, is that word 'flock.')

Again, the Epistle of James who is known to have been Christ's full brother killed by a special policeman's club in a street riot, has been reprinted and widely circulated by Socialists, in order to so broadcast their illogical theories of a universal brotherhood,

---

* "The ethics of Socialism are identical with the teachings of Christianity," *Encyclopaedia Britannica.*

founded upon enforced labor, regimentation of the herd, and majority votes.

Many modern cities are also infested with plausible epileptoid priestlings of unreason, like Dr. McGlynn, Professor Bemis, Hugh Price Hughes, W.T. Stead, Myron Reed, and Professor Herron of California. All these men are unrivaled masters in the art of persuasive declamation. They accept the New Testament as their text book and preach therefrom to morbid multitudes the atrocious and shallow gospel of equal rights, equal liberty, equal brotherhood, as the veritable omnific word, the newly discovered emancipating protocol of the Crucified (yet all-mighty) Don Quixote—the Saviour-god of Asia Minor—he who was born in a cattle-shed and died on a gallows.

A god begging his bread from door to door!—A god without a place to lay his head!—A god executed by order of a stipendary magistrate!—What an insane Idea—Is it an idea, or rather a wasting cranial disease? Talk about 'the heathen in his blindness' and superstitious madness in past ages! Why it is as childplay to the hysteric Idolatry of to-day—the deification of a Jew. The 'Divine Democrat' was executed upon a government gibbet, because the Rulers of Imperial Rome were more powerful men than he was. His strength, and that of his followers was not equal to theirs.

He died an abysmal failure—a Redeemer who did not redeem—a Saviour who did not save—a Messiah whipped like a calf—a slave-agitator deservedly destroyed for preaching a Falsehood—the monsterous gospel of Love, Brotherhood, Equality.

Even from the spiritual point of view, there is nothing whatever in his life or its after effects to show that 'The pale man upon the cross,' when he moaned and wept so bitterly, 'beheld any further down the Void, than those who gathered round to see him die.'

Of what use was that 'pale dreamer' to the iron-conditions that existed in the conquered and garrisoned Fortress of Jerusalem? For once the city mob were on the right trail, when they petitioned for the release of Bar Abbas, rather than the supple singer of a 'Sweet bye and bye.' Bar Abbas is described in 'the Scriptures' as a petty thief. He was really an armed insurgent leader—the slayer of Roman tax-gatherers—a guerrilla chief (like Rob Roy, Robin Hood, William Wallace, William Tell), who levied toll upon opulent Hebrews for patriotic purposes.

Had I been there that day, I also would have joined in the demand: 'Release Bar Abbus unto us.' Better one Bar Abbus than a thousand Christs.

Alas! Alas! O Gallilean! Thou art neither the Way, the Truth, nor the Light!

Reverting however, to Chicago's reverened Utopia-constructor. Thus waileth he with cajoling crudity: "The laws of social evolution, far from being the blind, barbarous, and brutal struggle for organic existence, consists in the physical, intellectual and moral well being of *all* the members of society, so constituted that the politico-ethical principles of Liberty, Equality, and Fraternity shall have the largest possible realization throughout the social organism. The main features of the condition of progress are christian churches, christian schools, christian governments, christian ethics and economics."

Another seductive but most malignant State Socialist (Henry George) roundly proclaims that "The salvation of society, the hope of the free, and full development of Humanity, is in the gospel of brotherhood, the gospel of Christ," and thereupon he proposes to make politicians the national rent-tax collectors, Administrators of everything in general, and all-round Distributors of State Pensions to 'the poor and needy.' Has not mankind had sufficient experience of what politicians are?—Those black-hearted creeping thieves and frauds. Their sting is deadlier than the bite of a cobra, and in the breath of their mouth there is—*death.* Curses be upon ye, O! ye Politicians, and upon all who advocate increasing your prerogatives!

Presidential candidates, from Jefferson to Lincoln (also their apish imitators) have generally indulged in equally shallow rodomontade, because it means votes and for votes, office-seekers would dress up in glowing language, and ray forth any devilish deception.

For two thousand years these effeminate superlatives have been trumpeted to the remotest corner of every Christian land, and yet (while enervating the morale of people), they have dismally failed to inaugurate the much foretold Earthly Paradise. They were preached by bare-foot monks at the inauguration of the Dark Ages, in order that those saintly lovers of the common people might creep into the administration of co-operative wealth and power. Now, the same general ideas are revived and dressed up (this time in politico-economic garb) by the eloquent agitator, in order that he may rule and plunder in the future, through the agency of the State; just as the priest once ruled and plundered through the equally rapacious agency of the Church.

When the Church triumphed the Dark Ages began, and when it is finally rooted out (together with all its social antennae) the

Heroic Age dawns once more. True heroes shall be born again as of old, for our women may yet be something more than rickety perambulating dolls and drug-stores in spectacles.

The 'Church' is the idol of the priestly parasite—The 'State' is the idol of the political parasite. Beware, O, America! that in escaping from the holy trickery of the monk, you fall not an easy prey to 'the loving kindness' of the politician. Even if the 'reformer' succeeds in re-establishing upon majority-votes, the dark tyranny of the 'greatest number'; we have this consolation to fall back upon, such organization must ultimately tumble down of its own weight, and then re-divide up into warring fragments. Nothing that is unnatural can last for long.

The Universal Church is no more; all we see of it now is jealous remnants. And the Universal State, the Social Democracy, the Economic Republic, the Brotherhood of Man, should they take practical form, are pre-ordained to similar failure. All they could do, would be to *postpone* the operation of survival of the fittest— drugging nations in temporary sedatives.

No matter how eagerly madmen may try to do it, there is no known process, whereby they can jump out of their own skins. Christian or socialist churches, paternalisms, schools, governments, administrations, ethics, and moralisms (even if genuinely Christian and Fraternal) would be wholly impotent to change the natural course of things and therefore powerless to command the survival of mental and physical cripples; even though those cripples were canonized saints for 'goodness,' and as the sands of the sea shore for number. Shrieking sentimentalism is indeed a feeble lever wherewith to overturn the immutable order of the Universe. It cannot do it. No! not if it were whooped till the crack of doom! Not even if it had a Lamb of God in every city, ready to be butchered each Friday afternoon, in order to make a Christian Holiday.

🐉 7 🐉

'Liberty, Equality, Fraternity,' those three great lights of Modern Democracies are three colossal Falsehoods—ignoble slave-shibboleths; impossible of actualization even if proclaimed by some superhuman Satan, followed by armed hosts of un-killable demons, all armed to the teeth with flaming swords, greek-fire, and dynamite cannon.

You may trace Equality in letters of silver on tablets of burnished gold, but without engineering a perpetual miracle, you cannot make it—true.

24

You may write Fraternity in blazing diamonds on walls of enduring granite, but without reversing the mechanism of the Universe, you cannot make it a fact.

And, though you enscroll Freedom on countless sheepskins and rivet statues of Liberty on every harbor-rock, yet with 'all the kings horses and all the kings men' one being born to be a hireling and a subordinate—*no* power can be free.

Can you build up a marble palace with mud and slime O! ye drivelling bedlamites? Can you raise up a conquerer from the dunghill, or make the stupid great? Can you manufacture heroes out of hogs O! ye snuffling 'Educated' swine?

'We can! We can! We can!' shrieketh the raging rhetoricians of the market place and the editorial mill. 'We can! We can!' bellows the herd as it stupidly pours through the slip-rails to the pithing pen. 'Yes, O! Yes! with the love of Jesus and our collection plate,' whines the soft-skinned preacher as he turns over the sybiline leaves of his Black-Art. 'Of a certainty, we can,' hisseth the plastic politician, the rattlesnake!—the hungry basilisk!—whose law making is more blighted than the breath of a simoom.

Thereupon, toward you, O! America! they, one and all, point the finger of pride! Toward you!

America! Where the politicians rage and the people imagine vain things!—and the dogs in the alleys are—baying at the moon!

Then, turn I away! Sadly! Sadly! Sadly! And I brush against a slave in copper riveted overalls, hurrying to his mill; and against another in gold chain and silken hat, hasting to his money-changing—and a lean woman in sordid rags, with a pile of lumber balanced upon her crown; and a splendid harlot in diamonds and brilliant plumage, rideth slowly by.

And the cattle in the slaughter-yard are lowing for their hay; and a draught mare, with a galled shoulder, lieth swollen and dead on the frozen paving blocks.—How nauseous it all is?

Loathsome! Loathsome! O, how loathsome!

Man is part and parcel of the animal kingdom and (notwithstanding Jefferson, Franklin, and Lincoln—Karl Marx, La Salle, and Liebknecht—Christ, Robespierre, and Rousseau—Hyndman, Tennyson, and Mazzini—Dr. Adler, Bebel, George and Isaiah—Bellamy, Gronlund, and W.T. Stead) he *cannot* escape from the draconic ordinances that despotically govern that kingdom and environ his being like an atmosphere on every side.

Altruism, meek and lowly self-abnegation, upon any extended scale is among predatory organisms (and all organisms are predatory) impossible to practice on pain of wholesale felo-de-se.

25

Every man is under an obligation to fight and bear his own burden. If he cannot do so, others cannot do his fighting or his burden-bearing and their own at the same time with reasonable safety to themselves. Therefore, he who finds it impossible to carry his own burden, had better sink down and die in his tracks than impose an additional load upon the shoulders of his kind hearted fellow strugglers. For then, *they* would be overloaded and consequently unable to fight successfully; *so all* might perish together.

Practical fraternal sympathy (upon any universal scale) has always had in the end a most destructive effect upon the internal structure of communities. Men will always love and cherish those that are near and dear to them; but when it is proposed to extend the circle of their 'near and dear ones' to all mankind, that is going rather too far. Indeed all must perish ignominiously if that foolish idea prevails. 'All' are even now enervating themselves, undermining their strength, by futile overexertion in that very direction. They are straining themselves to death, by endeavoring to carry an impossible load. The majority of men are born far too weak constitutionally for their conditions; and the few who do possess the necessary stamina and grit, will have quite enough to do in proving by deeds their fitness to survive, propogate, and possess. Many are projected—few are selected.

Yet altruism, wholesale self-renunciation—wholesale burden-bearing, for the sake of 'Outraged and Suffering Humanity,' is the maddening basis upon which 'our good Lord Jesus' and his demented imitators have erected their sporadic sociology—their Magnificent Satanism.

Does not simple business acumen whisper to us that man's chief occupation upon earth is to sustain himself. 'I mean subsist at any cost; you shall want ere I shall—business is business.' If men had sufficient personal initiative to think along these stern lines, there would be little use on earth for the theologian and 'the reformer;' those twin Mephistos who find their renown and grandeur in the abasement of mankind. The battle of life would then be so grim, terrible, and realistic; (so Trojan in fact) that those holy dissimulators and crafty deceivers would rapidly die off, or be eaten off; for in the clash of naked interests, the Best and Bravest *only* could possibly survive; and no one would ever dream of including them among the Best or Bravest.

Count Leo Tolstoi, undoubtedly the ablest modern expounder of primitive Christliness, in a much translated volume entitled: *Work While Ye Have Light,* writes thus: "Our Faith tells us that bliss is to be found, not in resistance, but in submission; not in riches, but in giving everything away;...we have not quite succeeded in casting off every habit of violence and property."

To the most inept understanding, could any proposition be placed in a clearer light? Is it not as simple as 'rolling off a log,' that the individual who even attempts to become a true and honest Christian must become like a tame sheep? What a sublime Ideal? How heroic?

The bliss of a sheep! How superlatively delightful? How divinely glorious? And a Jew as the Good Shepherd, who leadeth his lambs "to green pastures, and quiet resting places, the pleasant waters by." For two thousand years, or so, His fleecy flocks have been fattening themselves up with commendable diligence—for the shearing-shed and the butcher's-block.

Let any nation throw away all 'habits of violence,' and before long it must cease to exist as a nation. It will be laid under tribute—it will become a province, a satrapy. It will be taxed and looted in a thousand different ways.

Let any man abandon all property, also all overt resistance and aggression and behold, the first sun will scarcely have sunk down in the west before he is a bondservant, a tributary, a beggar, or—a corpse.

Property is necessary to the complete and free development of personality, and therefore human animals should somehow obtain a full and fair proportion thereof at any cost—or perish in the attempt; for he who cannot possess himself of property is much better buried out of sight. Our cities are literally honeycombed with treasure caverns, heaped up with gold, title-deeds, silver and instruments of credit: our valleys and our mountains are actually bubbling with wealth untold; and yet, poor miserable 'servants of Christ' pass idly by. Men, they call themselves! I call them—castrates.

If Tolstoi's obsequious principles are derived from the Sermon on the Mount, then who can deny but that the Sermon on the Mount is a sermon unto decay and slavery? If they are derived from the Golden Rule and if the Golden Rule is the word of God, then can it be doubted that the word of God is the word of Fraud? There is far too much of this ghastly 'goodness' in the nation, far and away too much. It is time men who *can* think began to emancipate themselves, and consider the fact that: Morals, laws and decalogues were made by liars, thieves and rogues.

All good citizens however are hereby warned and solemnly advised, not to smash-up the Ten Commandments—not to burn up the Golden Rule—not to break-up the Moral Law—for that would be terribly wicked! terribly! On the other hand they must all obey all Law implicitly (no matter how it originated) and be sure (above everything) to order themselves lowly and reverently before executive officers of the Law; even if in doing so, they are deprived of their Property, and their Liberty for ever. Obedience, you see, is of God 'who so loveth the world' but Disobedience is horrible and of the Devil, and the Devil is a frightful rascal, who has not the slightest respect for anybody or anything: not even the American Constitution. Let us curse the Devil then and obey—the Law.

Liberty is honestly definable, as a state of complete bodily and mental self-mastership (which includeth the possession of property; also defensive weapons) and thorough-going Independence from all official coercion or restraint. Liberty in the conventional sense is a miserable Lie.

To be independent is synonymous with proprietorship. To be property-less, and unarmed, is the condition of actual dependence and servitude. Unarmed citizens are always enslaved citizens, always. Liberty without property is a myth, a nursery tale, believable only by babbling babies, and 'fools-i-th-forest'—fools th' city also. "Liberty *regulated* by Law" is, in practice, tyranny of the darkest and foulest description; because so impersonal. There are numerous worthy, reasonable, and practical methods whereby individual tyrants may be removed; but a tyranny 'regulated by Law' is only removable by one method—the sword in the hands of men who are not afraid to use it, or to have it used against them: that is to say—the Sword in the hands of the Strongest.

During the whole course of human history, there is not upon record one authentic instance wherein a subjugated people has ever regained property-holding Liberty, without first butchering its tyrants (or its tyrants' armed slaves in battle) thereafter confiscating to its own use the lands and realized property that previously had been in the possession of its defeated foes and masters. This statement is made with cool deliberation and aforethought. Let it be disproved by any *one* credible example to the contrary, and the Author is prepared to forfeit 50,000 ounces of pure gold and enough 'dimes and dollars' to erect in Chicago a bronze statue of 'Our Blest Redeemer' (crown of thorns and all) 100 cubits higher than the Masonic Temple. This offer is strictly bona-fide and shall remain open until 1906, so that philosophers, editors, statesmen, divines (and other accomplished liars) may have enough time to blind themselves, wading through National Archives, and the putrid rubbish heaps that men call Public Libraries. Should some or all of said Mutual Admiration Society maniac-geniuses go blind, also deaf, dumb, and silly: this wicked old world may probably whoop with delight—should it happen to hear of the fact.

 9

During the three years of Christ Jesus's peripatetic trampings, he never *said* anything that had not been better said a thousand times before, by Dervishes, Spell-binders and Mahatmas. Neither did he *do* anything that had not previously been better done, by the jugglers and wonder-workers of Egypt, India and Assyria. Not a few of his 'miracles' are to this day part of the ordinary stock-in-trade of fortune-telling gypsies, third-class strolling players, and charlatans in general.

The very phrase He uses to sum-up and memorize His patent Cure-all, was undoubtedly stolen (directly or indirectly) from Plato, the Rig Veda, or Confucius. The Golden Rule is not only a snare and a tangle, but it also is—a literary piracy.

'He raised the dead,' you indignantly protest: and even *supposing* that he did, wherein is the positive advantage? What is gained by restoring vitality to the decomposing corpse of an animal that may be so easily duplicated—an animal that is a positive nuisance, numerically? What is the "good" of breathing the 'breath of life' into an odorous winding-sheet-full of maggots and mouldy bones? Are there not plenty of animalculae on Earth, without dragging them out of tombs? (Especially are there not plenty of leprous Asiatics?) Death and destruction are necessary to the health of this world, and therefore as natural, and lovable, as birth and life. Only priests and born cowards moan and weep over dying. Brave men face it with approving nonchalance.

"Come lovely and soothing Death, undulate around
the world. Serenely Arriving! Arriving! In the day,
in the night; to all, to each. Sooner or later,
delicate Death."*

He fed the hungry—but to what end, I say? Why should a famishing multitude be fed by a god? And that too, in a land said to be flowing with milk and honey! Would not such a mob be far better dead? Would not Napoleon with his cosmic 'whiff of grape-

---

* Walt Whitman's "Ode to Death."

29

shot' be just the right man for such an occasion? From the harmonious nature of things, it is clear that men were intended to feed themselves by their own personal exertions or perish like dogs. He, therefore, who 'feeds the hungry' is really encouraging poltroonery (which includeth all other crimes) for men who quietly starve within reach of abounding plenty are—all poltroons.

'He clothed the naked,' you shriek; and why it may be asked should 'the naked' be clothed—they being able bodied? What right have they to broadcloth and fine linen? If men possess not enough sense to clothe themselves (in a literal Weaving Mill of inexhaustible looms) why should a 'God'—the son of a ghost, come down from Cloudland (via a Jewess maiden's womb) to robe such grovelling, miserable hounds in swaddling cloths, made of cotton or wool? 'Clothing the naked' is purely—a business affair.

Here, it may be suggested en-passant—is the wearing of garments, in itself, a natural and necessary condition of adult existence? It certainly does not render the 'human form divine' more healthy or more beautiful to gaze upon (although it may prevent Tenderlings from perishing of cold). Was it really intended that the man-animal *only*, should wrap itself up, from birth to death in layer over layer of disease-breeding rags? Was there not a secret vital strength in the wind and rain and storms that whirled around our forefathers' giant limbs and shaggy brows? All ethnic legends tell us that our first parents were most elegantly attired in glorious sunshine and gaudy fresh air. Who ever saw a Cherubim painted in pointed shoes, pantaloons, cuffs, collars and overcoat; or a smirking angel in bloomers, steel-ribbed corsets and a delicate little 'O! dear me! how awfully awful! style? Clothing serves most effectively to hide the abominable physical deformity of modern men and women, just as superficial educationalisms serve to hide their dwarfed minds. If they were to perambulate around in the nude, even the street curs would bark at them out of sheer terror. Indeed, they would be more hideous to the eye than the stuffed scarecrow that adorns a relative's harrowed field: and at which our old dog "Danger" generally barks himself into hysterics over, whenever he gets off the chain.

What a horrible sight a crowd of free and independent electors would be, all sitting in solemn conclave, sucking their thumbs; absorbing political opiates and divine euthanasia? Just think of it! (Even Carlyle the dyspeptic would faint at the sight.) The very conception of such a saddening horror makes one ill. It would be as if they all had just emerged from a tomb—a tomb of wool and cotton and leather.

Physical distortion and mental malformation are the direct result of two thousand years of bad-breeding: that is to say, of

Mongrelism, of Democracy, of Equality, of Mody-and-Sankeyism. Christian-ism, originating in the despairful and fallacious philosophy of a Crucified Wanderer (suffering from acute *morbus sacer*) is now developed into an organized and world-wide conspiracy of Clericals, Politicals and Decadents directed en-masse; with Jesuitic cunning against all the primitive and Heroic Virtues.

Our clean-skinned 'heathenish' ancestors with all their vital forces unimpaired, were really the nobler type of animal. We on the other hand, with our corrupt, irresolute, civilized hearts, our trembling nerves, our fragile anemic constitutions, are actually the lower, the viler type—notwithstanding the baseless optimism that courtly rhymers drivel into their "Heirs of all the ages," etc., etc.

No People can long retain hardihood and independence, whose minds become submissive to a False Ideal.

🜨 10 🜨

Blessed are the Strong for they shall possess the earth—Cursed are the Weak for they shall inherit the yoke. Blessed are the Powerful for they shall be reverenced among men—Cursed are the Feeble for they shall be blotted out.

Blessed are the Bold for they shall be masters of the world— Cursed are the Humble for they shall be trodden under hoofs. Blessed are the Victorious for victory is the basis of Right— Cursed are the Vanquished for they shall be vassals forever.

Blessed are the battle-blooded, Beauty shall smile upon them— Cursed are the Poor-in-Spirit, they shall be spat upon. Blessed are the Audacious for they have imbibed true wisdom—Cursed are the Obedient for they shall breed Creeplings.

Blessed are the iron-handed, the unfit shall flee before them— Cursed are the haters of battle, subjugation is their portion. Blessed are the Death-defiant, their days shall be long in the land—Cursed are the Feeble-brained, for they shall perish amidst plenty.

Blessed are destroyers of False-hope, they are true Messiahs— Cursed are the God-adorers, they shall be shorn sheep. Blessed are the Valiant for they shall obtain great treasure—Cursed are the believers in Good and Evil for they are frighted by shadows.

Blessed are they who believe in Nothing—never shall it terrorize their minds—Cursed are the 'lambs of God,' they shall be bled 'whiter than snow.' Blessed is the man who hath powerful

31

enemies, they shall make him a hero—Cursed is he who 'doeth good' unto others, he shall be despised.

Blessed the man whose foot is swift to serve a friend, he is a friend indeed—Cursed are the organizers of Charities, they are propagators of plagues. Blessed are the Wise and Brave for in the Struggle they shall win—Cursed are the Unfit for they shall be righteously exterminated.

Blessed are the sires of Noble Maidens, they are the salt of the earth—Cursed the mothers of strumous Tenderlings for they shall be shamed. Blessed are the Mighty-minded for they shall ride the whirl-winds—Cursed are they who teach Lies for Truth, and Truth for Lies, for they are—abomination.

Blessed are the Unmerciful, *their* posterity shall own the world—Cursed are the famous Wiselings, their seed shall perish off the earth. Thrice cursed are the Vile for they shall serve and suffer.

Contrast *this* with an orthodox Sermonette—one that is repeated every seventh day, in thousands of sacred sanctuaries by consecrated black-robed clericals, who have been specially trained from boyhood to weepfully, unctiously rehearse the same with upturned eyes and skillful snuffle or in classic diction, sounding, sonorous, na! sublime—as suits the occasion.

Dearly Beloved bretheren!!!

—Gawd answers all who kneel and pray, is a Trewth accepted day by day. Behold! their bright and joyful lot, who've faith in what Christ Jesu taught!

If you empty pockets and tables bare, demand ye not your natural share; that would be wrong; but, creep and sigh and 'you'll go to heaven when you die.'

For the meek and humble who obey, there's a happy land, far, far away; but a fearsome, fiery, brimstone pit, shall melt their marrow, who won't—submit.

If foemen smite you on one cheek, turn round the other, tearful, meek; if perjured knaves your votes betray: come 'wicked sinners' kneel and—pray.

If Hebrews fleece and flay your hide, heaven's gates for you, shall open wide; Christ your Shepherd, won't lead astray, O! lambs of Gawd! come bleat and pray.

If bruised and beaten, shorn and sold, you're sure of stalls in your Father's fold; but—robbers rob, or rulers slay! Hell roast your souls for ever and aye.

If elected persons invade your wealth, with bribes and lies or deadly stealth, and threat your bones with bannered host: Chirst is your refuge and the Holy Ghost.

32

You'll triumph thus 'in the dawning years' hope on! toil on! in this vale of tears—sing, "Rock of Ages cleft for me, O! let me hide myself in thee."

BOLDLY STAND ERECT

Jewish books are for the Jew,
    And Jew Messiahs, too.
But if you're not of Jewish blood,
    How can they be for you?

To make an Idol of a book,
    Is poison for the brain;
A dying God upon a cross
    Is reason gone insane.

Beware of all the Holy books
    And all the creeds and schools,
And every law that man has made
    And all the golden rules.

"Laws" and "rules" imposed on you
    From days of old renown,
Are not intended for your "good"
    But for your crushing down.

Then dare to rend the chains that bind
    And to yourself be true.
Dare to liberate your mind,
    From all things, old and new.

Always think your own thought,
    All other thoughts reject;
Learn to use your own brain
    And boldly stand erect.

3

THE SPINNING OF THE WEB

Just as the spider weaves his silky web, to lure flies into the larder of his banqueting hall, in order that he may diet at his leisure, pick the flesh off their bones, so, deceitful Ideals are cunningly woven by dextrous political spiders, to capture and exploit swarms of human flies.

What are the grandiose paragraphs of the Declaration of Independence, but the weft and woof of a dazing spider-web? And what are the American People but the flies that have been cleverly entagled in its gossamer meshes? For over a century this 'Declaration' has been the parchment divinity of all public orators, from the curbstone dervish at the street corner, to our Elective Monarch in the White House. Every 4th of July, Americans habitually scream themselves hoarse over its sounding generalities: making the welkin ring with tin-horns, giant fire-crackers, flag-idolatry, brass bands, toy pistols and herd-bellowing generally. Although the great majority of them are mental and physical dwindlings, poverty-striken, and property-less, yet how insanely they delight in amusing a sardonic world with their locquacious flambuoyant charlatanry. 'We are sovereigns and equals' is their everlasting Barmecide chorus. 'Sovereigns and Equals!'

In all lunatic asylums may be found inmates who fancy themselves kings and queens, and lords of the earth. These sorrowful creatures, if only permitted to wear imaginary crowns and issue imaginary commands, are the most docile and harmless of all maniacs.

As for the American People of to-day: is not their written constitution but a cunningly constructed straight-jacket—their moral codes, padded prison cells—their statute laws handcuffs and leg-irons—their Captains of Industry keepers and turnkeys in clever disguise? One hundred years ago they ostensibly commenced 'independent' operations with the richest continent

34

on earth as their private property—their subscribed capital; and during the whole of that period, have they not been as busy as so many relays of draught beasts-of-burden, pumping the tremendous natural wealth out of their home soil, and pouring it over-sea, into the cess-pools of Europe?

Is not that the work of lunatics? They smashed and splintered the wooden political yoke of an English king and then proceded to rivet around their necks a brand new yoke of bolted steel, which they forged especially to fit themselves; and which they dignified under the name of "Constitutional Freedom."

Is not that also the work of lunatics? Cursed indeed are the harnessed ones! Cursed are they even though their harness be home made—even although it tinkle musically with silver bells— aye! even though every buckle and link and rivet thereof be made of solid gold.

How absurd of men to hurrah over their 'glorious political liberty' who have not even been able to retain possession of the substantial products of their own laboriousness. After a century of 'constitutional progress,' ten per cent of the population are absolute owners of ninety-two percent of *all* the property.

Now, O reader, Are not *these things* the outward and visible sign of organic dementia?

The Declaration of Independence commences by proclaiming an unctious falsehood, a black degrading self-evident lie—a lie which no one could possibly believe but a born fool. With insolent effrontery it brazenly proclaims as 'a self evident truth' that 'all men are created equal' and that they are 'endowed by their 'Creator'* with certain 'inalienable' rights'—rights which it thereupon proceeds to define in canting phraseology, imbecile and florid as it is false.

Indeed the mock-heroic preamble of this rhetorical pronounciamento is but a cunningly constructed piece of blague deliberately intended to deceive and betray. It consists of a patchwork of plagiarized catchwords, annexed wholesale from the ravings of seventeenth-century Levellers, crazed puritanic Mattoids and eighteenth-century cretinous French Jacobins: all mixed up and jumbled together with long rigamarole of semi-meaningless pretty phrases, culled mostly from an old time melodrama.

---

* A mythical airy being who roams about Eternity manufacturing Things out of No-Things—A fable.

The Declaration of Independence has less real meaning for present conditions than a bottled-up Indian war-whoop of the same period would have, if uncorked now. It is a back-number, musty high smelling, and worm-eaten: only fit for the walls of a museum or the brain-cells of—a daft philosopher.

Its ethical, and most of its political conclusions are shams, deceptions, and cold-blooded dishonesties—incandescent Lies—glorified, belauded, printed in letters of gold, but nevertheless—Lies.

Indeed it has always been considered a piece of amusing mockery by those who really understood the secret intent for which it was originally constructed, viz: as a lasso for the bellowing Herds, that, about one hundred years ago were beginning to run wild, and escape from their herdsmen, and herdsmen's stock-whip, in this (then) boundless New World.

To all contemporary demagogues, the high-sounding phraseology of the "Declaration" is as honey from paradise. Everywhere its seductive abstractions are the Avatars of anarchism, communism, republicanism, and scores of other zymotic convulsionisms. Why then should sane men continue giving lip-service to this subtle deception? Why should they, by their silence, acquiesce in the malefic efforts of Organic Weaklings (instigated by prattlers of false philosophy) to enforce by electioneering mass-pressure an impossible and hideous Equality Ideal?

Every national appeal is *now* made, not to the Noblest and Best, but to the riff-raff—the slave-hordes—who possess less intelligence than night-owls. All that is brave, honorable, heroic, is ignored tacitly, for fear of offending the deified Herd, 'the Majority.' "Equality of conditions" is *its* debasing shibboleth and *verily* he who has temerity enough to spit upon Equality is liable to be honored to death.

The 'Voice of the People' can only be compared to the fearsome shrieks of agony, that may now and then be heard, issuing forth from the barred windows of a roadside madhouse. 'The voice of God!' Alas! Alas!

𝄢 3 𝄢

There are two methods whereby masterful ambitious men may hold any population in a state of ordered subjectivity. The first and by far the most honerable method is through an irresistible and highly-trained standing army, ready to deploy anywhere; with mechanical precision at a telegraphic nod in order to lay down the

Law at the cannons mouth and sweep away all dangerous opposition.

The second and cheaper method is, first of all to innoculate those intended to be exploited with some poisonous political soporific, superstition, or theoria; something that operating insidiously, hypodermically, may render them laborious, meek, and tractable.

The latter plan has ever proved itself most effective because Aryan populations that would fight to the last gasp against undisguised military despotism, may be induced to passively submit to any indignity or extortion, if their brains are first carefully soaked in some Abstract Lie.

At the period of the War of Independence, North America was far too wide, far too sparsely settled, and far too poor in concentrated wealth to be effectively ruled and plundered upon the standing army principle: either by King George or the successful Junta of power-wielding Revolutionists.

Hamilton, Hancock, Jefferson, Adams, Madison, Henry, and all the vested material interests that stood a solid phalanx behind those voluble patriots cast about for some safer method of ruling the minds of the uninformed but extremely valorous yeomanry, backwoodsmen and mountaineers.

After mature consideration they determined to lull and lure the armed peasantry back again into a condition of blissful somnolence, by installing into their newly aroused minds, false but seductive political Idealisms, as subtle supplements to the fallacious, and equally delusive (but pre-existent) religionisms and moralisms. This cunning plot worked like a charm, for Equality of Rights seemed to puritanic minds the logical outcome of that other hoary old lie—'Equality before God.' ("What a set of damned rascals they were!" was Governor Morris's terse, rugged, but ever memorable description of the Congress of smart Corruptionists, that adopted and formally proclaimed those famous and fatal Abstractions.)

Thereupon the Sword of Power, that conquered on the battlefield, was carefully hidden away out of sight and 'Constitutionalism' invoked to aid in the re-harnessing of the Conquerers of Cornwallis, by their new masters. The old system of Jurisprudence and Government (founded on naked force) were cleverly retained even amplified and at the same time the white skinned populations were cunningly proclaimed 'free and equal.' Never having enjoyed genuine personal freedon (except on the Indian border), being for the most part descendants of hunted-out European starvelings and fanatics (defeated battlers), they now stupidly thought that they had won Freedom at last by the patent device of selecting a complete outfit of new tax-gatherers every fourth year.

When we look back upon the childlike faith in Constitutionalism, displayed by our Revolutionary Fathers together with their infantile republican specifics for the redemption of mankind, we cannot help smiling. At every general election, since 1776, Americans have voted solidly for increasing the despotic authority of their elective rulers and task-masters. Personal liberty is very nearly unknown (except in the newspaper) and any citizen who dares to think in direct opposition to the dogma of the Majority, does so at the risk of his life, if he thinks too loudly.

Indeed, men of initiative and enterprise are now in the regular habit of purchasing immunity from Communal molestation by bribing legislatures and officials upon a wholesale scale. The State is a blackmail agency.

Enterprises necessitating state-permits and large preliminary expenditures of capital, cannot be safely undertaken, until elective satraps (Aldermen, Judges, Governors, Congressmen, Presidents, Senators, etc.), have first negotiated a percentage "rake-off." Neither life nor property is safe from the malignance, revenge or greed of government officials or their confederates. He who would assert himself in this Republic, under present conditions, must be a man of unscrupulous acumen and shrewdness. He must know the exact price of every 'patriot,' with whom business brings him in contact and be ready to pay it without demur, nay—with an appearance of hearty enthusiasm: otherwise it will go hard with him. Should he be a poor man, his chances in life are infinitesimal; so long as he is conscientious. No citizen can 'call his soul his own,' who dares to openly attack the administrative scoundrelism—scoundrelism based securely upon purchaseable majority votes. Those thievish official speculators of Turkey, China, Persia and Morocco, would hang their heads in utter shame at their own clumsy methods of robbery, if they once beheld the magnificent mechanism and finesse wherewith American politicians enrich themselves by bleeding the treasuries, stealing public lands, and sweating the revenues.

Indeed, *our* Grand Vizers (heaven bless them) not only plunder living generations, but they even make Futurity contribute to their hungry rapacity.

Their schemes of financial legerdemain are of unparalleled brilliance and grandeur. They borrow thousands of millions upon National Credits from the Userers, and then proceed to apportion the money unto each other, under the elaborate pretence of needful public expenditure, redeeming the currency, etc., etc.

In order that the Jew may be secured in his usurous 'shent-per-shent,' oppressive taxes are laid on the Peasantry wherewith to pay the annual interest charge upon the Bonded Millions. All of these tributes are collectable (in appreciating gold) at the point of the Supreme Court's bayonet. However, military assistance is very seldom needed to enforce the tax-collectors demands, because most Americans are exceptionally docile and 'good.' No need of coercion with a palsied people, ever eager to obey the slightest nod of their Masters.

America! America! Never shall you realize the true meaning of thorough-going Independence and Self-Proprietorship, until an American Cromwell, or an American Ceaser has signed the death-warrant of an American King. The Executive that sells his people into bondage is a Public Enemy; whether he be an elective Monarch or a hereditary King. Such a Scoundrel and Traitor has no rights that property-holding Freemen are bound to respect: no not one. By accepting the gold of Public Plunderers, he makes himself an Ishmaelite. His hand is against every man's heart and every man's property. Therefore every man's hands should be uplifted against him.

In days not long gone by, men of our Race have hung bribe-takers with scant ceremony; and even rolled the heads of Kings into the executioner's basket.

If we are not to be robbed now of everything we possess and reduced to conditions of absolute State servitude, we must not shrink from doing so again.

Despotism, if it is to be overthrown, must be fought with its own weapons, and the vilest of Despotisms are ever founded upon Majority Votes.

As for the 'Common People,' they are energetically chasing shadowy paternalisms, and allowing their substance to be 'appropriated' on a gigantic scale. They are living in a fool's paradise of 'progress,' and 'peaceful industrial evolution' as the cant phrases go. Some of these days they may possibly wake up (when too late) and discover, with alarm and astonishment, that all their mock iambics have been of no avail against the insidious growth of centralized Oligarchic Hebraism, ballot-box desolation, and industrial imperialism.

Americans have yet to learn, that each generation must fight out its own good fight, and not rely for the preservation of its hardihood and independence upon the moth-eaten parchments nor on fraudulent statesmen, now in the graveyard—statesmen who spent their petty babblesome lives, not in doing heroic things, but in founding and enthroning the abominations that afflict us all to-day like a palsy. Our natural hero-worship badly wants reconstruction.

Many years after the "Declaration" was issued, our written Constitution was constructed with much voluble sophistry and mimic strife. That document considered as a whole, is the most cunningly worded and at the same time most terrible instrument of Government and Mastership that any Anglo-Teutonic tribe has ever yoked itself up under. Pretending to 'grant' liberty and self-government, it practically annihilates both. Under the show of "guaranteeing" personal independence and civil rights, it has organized an elective tyranny, wherein the mob-monarch possesses more arbitrary authority, than any dynastic despot since the days of Darius or Balschazzar.

The highest crime *is* actually 'written in the highest law of the land.'

"Thus, did the great Guile-Masters,
Their toils and their tangles set;
And, as wide as was the water:
So wide was woven the net."

Indeed the written Constitution of our Republic is a monstrous mechanical contrivance, that bids fair (when once it has got properly under way) to squeeze the very heart out of all the Best Elements in America.

Our Federal Government may be very appropriately compared to a pirate ship cleverly disguised as a friendly armed cruiser; convoying a fleet of peaceful merchantmen loaded with an immense treasure and 70,000,000 passengers. When it first came to their "assistance," it was—O! so kindly! so affectionate! so full of loving regard for its intended prey, for the welfare and bon-voyage of its quarry. Now however that its forty-five ships of state are out in the open ocean, and absolutely at its mercy, it strips off its decoy rig; hoists the 'Death's-head-and-bloody-bones,' opens its hidden portholes, runs out its round-lipped broadsides, and yells through its editorial speaking-trumpets: "Heave too there, or you'll be blown out of the water."

Thus it will be seen that the Jesuitic 'Evangel of Equality' has proved itself a tremendous success. It seduced the American

People into a feeling of contentment and security till their 'bonds' and fetters were properly forged, polished, and neatly riveted on.

Well fashioned, indeed, was the Net!—A splendid spider web it has proved itself, and withal, needful.

Under the hypnotic spell of a 'free and equal' dream, Americans have been hustled into a convict-prison of laboriousness to piratical masters a thousand times more terrible and more unyielding than any history can describe. All that is now left of Liberty is its name, and the harmless privilege the common people have of scolding their Proprietors in vulgar editorial diatribes at or about election times. Occasionally they do descend into the streets, indulging in sanguinary vociferations upon the same general principle that impels a mangy cur to howl most dismally—if struck with a brick.

The conflict between the masters and the helots is over for the present and the masters having conquered, are in possession of the booty and the field. Hark! the songs of victory—the flap of the battle-pennons!

Indeed, considering all the circumstances, the common people are 'lost souls'—no matter what they now do they must remain in hell. Their position is that of a worm trying to escape from its hole in a heated burning log; if it runs to the right it runs into heat and smoke; if it runs to the left, it runs into blazes. A few minutes more and—it is roasted alive.

Even should America's servile multitudes appeal to the arbitrament of Physical Force, they cannot possibly win. Possessing neither the strength, courage, brains, arms, money, nor leaders: they must be blown into eternal fragments by their masters' highly trained artillerists, and scientific destroyers.

 6

The citadel of Power is now consolidated and prepared with the most approved armaments to repel any assault, no matter how well sustained. The nation is intersected in all directions, with iron highroads and splendid waterways, whereon armies and navies may be moved from city to city, with facility and dread effect. The war of Secession (or rather the war for the annihilation of Self-Government) demonstrated conclusively that a Centralized Authority, resting on herd-votes of the vulgar and fanatic, is (in practice) military Absolutism. There is no other Power in the land that can effectively hold it in check. The Czar of Russia possesses less actual authority than our Federal Government. With a standing army in the hollow of its hand, it can do exactly as it pleases, i.e., if it can collect enough revenue to purchase 'statesmen' and pay the salaries of its praetorian cohorts.

Most Americans are *only now* beginning to perceive these things, but they were foreseen (and also foretold in part) by clear-sighted individuals before the Constitution itself was formally enthroned.

To-day all the old sphinx questions are up again for solution. No man of balanced sense can honestly believe that these problems are to be settled by ballot-box stuffing or Editorialism. Settled they must be upon 'the good old rule, the simple plan,' and thereafter settled and re-settled again and again; for, there is no finality in social adjustments and there should not be. Material strength is the basis of all human greatness and material strength must 'settle' the tyranny of the greatest number; probably with fire and steel. All other theories are chimeras—lies—delusions—make-believe and of no account.

The Philosophy of Power has slumbered long, but whenever men of sterling worth are found, it must again sweep away the ignoble dollar-damned Pedlarisms of to-day and openly as of old, dominate the destiny of an emancipated and all-conquering race.

What is viler than a government of slaves and usurous Jews? What is grander than a government of the Noblest and Best—who have proved their Fitness on the plains of Death?

Cromwell and his Ironsides—Ceaser and his Legions shall be born again, and the thunderous thread of Sulla's fierce destroyers shall roll and rumble amid the fire and glare and smoke of crumbling contitutionalisms: 'as it was in the beginning, is now, and ever shall be'—warfare without end.

Yawping politicians may harangue base city mobs of hirelings and Christians with "Alas, poor Yorick!" rhapsody, as if struggle and strife were the evil of all evils. Figures of speech, however, cannot breathe the breath of life into feline philosophies that never have had the slightest foundation in Fact. The survival of the Fittest—the Toughest is the logic of events and of all time. They who declare otherwise are blind. The chief point is this: that Fitness must honestly demonstrate itself not by ignoble theft and theory but by open conflict as per Darwin's law of battle.

How can citizens be honestly described as free and equal who are not, who never were, "free and equal" in any reasonable sense of the phrase? How can they be even considered *men*, whose whole lives are governed by cast-iron regulations; whose every movement is circumscribed and restrained by penal threats— even whose secret thoughts are in a constant state of silent repression?

42

It is no apology whatever to affirm that the People themselves enact all laws the are *commanded* to obey. Even that statement is a falsity and if it were true, it would not justify majority Dictatorship or any other kind of Dictatorship.

The Constitution under which all other laws are born, was accepted, not by us but by bewigged individuals who are long since rotten. We are ruled, in fact, by cadavers—the inhabitants of tombs.

Why should agreements made by coffined dead men, bind and mortgage living, pulsing, breathing beings?

Their bones have long ago mouldered into ozone and fertilizers, who drew up and signed the Bill of Rights, Magna Charta, the Sermon on the Mount, the Declaration of Independence, our Glorious Constitution, etc., etc. Rotten are the brains that concocted them and the fingers that signed and sealed them. Equally rotten are their irrational and infantile philosophies. Rotten also in their heart, are the men who obey *under compulsion* voices from the tomb.

No doubt these old documents served their purpose at the time, but 'new occasions teach new duties,' and new ages require, not only new leaders, but new deeds.

Again, most Acts of Congress are the Machiavellian work of eminent rogues, curse those whose very names are almost forgotten except by partisan chroniclers, and printers of public school histories.

As for the Common Law, it is an inheritance from those interesting old days, when Saxon and Norman earls (they were genuine noblemen then, for they had won their position by risking their lives in battle) administered 'Justice' direct, per media of knotted clubs, hilted knives, and long handled cleavers. That was the only kind of 'Law' understood by our 'uncivilized' forefathers, for *they* had not been 'educated' into the profound conviction that governments and laws 'derive all their just powers from the consent of the governed.' Such an expression would have sent them into convulsions, and he who uttered it would be considered—a most excellent fool.

No doubt our ancestors were somewhat rude in their manners, somewhat deficient in sweetness and culture but in matters of frozen fact they were decidedly logical. They did not sneak to public meetings and swagger about 'Liberty,' 'Justice,' and 'Equality of Opportunity,' or 'Rights of Man,' when they knew full well that not only their lives, but everything they nominally possessed was 'by leave' of their conquerers and proprietors. They accepted their position pro-tem, and when again ready, honestly re-entered the doom-ring to test anew their Fate.

It they could come alive again how these old Pirates and Freebooters would stare in shame and scorn at the sight of their 'tenderfoot' posterity, walking up in solemn, horny-handed, hump-backed procession in shoddy rags, before an idol-altar called a ballot-box, dropping into its gilded maw, printed invocations for Justice, Mercy, Liberty, "Peace in our time O! Lord!"—Protection—Cheap Money—'more laws! more laws! more laws!' How our blonde, clean-limbed ancestors would guffaw? Indeed, they would probably keep on guffawing, till they guffawed themselves to death again.

"Oh!" they would say: "to think that our seed should have sunk so low!"

❀ 7 ❀

But, Equality before the Law is all we mean, whimpers the everlasting sophist—the cunning liar! Let us see! By what rational method can any two litigants be placed in a position of unconditional 'Equality before the Law?' First of all, plaintiff and defendant always possess totally different physical and mental characteristics, different personal magnetisms and—different sized bank balances. Also, all judges, juries, and legal officials are unequals in temperament, ability, courage and honesty. Each one has his own peculiar idiosyncracies, prejudices, inferiorities, superstitions, and—price. Each again, may be more or less dishonest and more or less subject to financial pressure or caste bias. No two men are born alike: each one being literally born under his own peculiar star, formed of different material, swayed by different ideals, educated and molded in a different mill, by a different process.

Even if all tribunals of Justice were founded upon blind Impartiality and administered free of cost, it will be plainly seen that 'Equality before the Law' remains a mere chimera, a dream, and of no real value. 'Equality before the Law,' is just a meaningless catchword, something like that famous jesuitism— 'Liberty regulated by Law.'

Statute Law may formally confer equal rights and privileges upon unequal citizens, but it cannot enforce itself—it must execute its mandate through human media and that media is full up to the brim with superiorities, inferiorities, and inequalities.

No legalism has ever been devised that Strength can not drive its coach and four through and it is a popular proverb (in all lands) that somehow, there is 'one law for the rich and another for the poor.' Indeed the poor can *never* be placed upon an equality with the rich—not even by the pillage of the rich.

44

Whether they are the Fittest or not, the present proprietors of Wealth should never permit themselves to be plundered, without a savage struggle.

Sooner or later, the hour of this struggle in its acute form shall arrive, but the Rich must not dread it. If they prepare in time, the result shall not only justify their mastership, but render it impregnable—if they are Fit. To be respected and secure, Aristocracies must rest themselves upon Sworded Might, not upon paper-credits, consols, and bond issues.

Should the Oppulents be conquered and pillaged, that in itself will be conclusive evidence that they are neither the Fittest nor the Best. Upon this earth there is no such thing as Equal Justice.

All legal tribunals are based, not upon ideal concepts of Justice and Fair Play, but upon effective armed Strength. This is a truism. Robbery under arms, laid the corner stone of every Court House in Christiandom and elsewhere. How then can the robbers and the robbed—the eagle and the pigeon—the chicken and the hawk be placed in positions of genuine equilibrium before removable officials, specially paid and appointed, to 'vindicate the Law'—that is to give forcible effect to the Dicta of the Strongest?

All judges are authorized avengers armed to the teeth and all hangmen are licensed assassins, trained to kill. These words are not spoken in disparagement. Assassins and avengers! Ha! If that be so. . . .

Truly they that "seek the Lord" *do* suffer hunger but—lions seek for prey.

When an army of occupation settles down upon an enemy's territory, it issues certain rules of 'procedure' for the orderly transference of the property and persons of the conquered into the absolute possession and unlimited control of the conquerers. These 'rules of procedure' may at first take shape as orders issued by military generals; but after a time they develop themselves into Statute Books, Precedents, and Constitutions. Indeed *all* Law is now and ever has been, the mandate of successful belligerents or rather the mandate of the few masterful personalities that ever inspire them.

Equality before the Law, is thus a contradiction in terms for Law itself is an incarceration of Inequality. It is true only in the subjective sense, that all who *obey* the Law are equally the servants of those who make it or cause it to be made.

Drum-head court martials are really Law Courts in embryo. Congresses and Parliaments are merely committees of rapacious tax-gatherers. Legislators may describe themselves as 'representatives of the people,' but that is only a cunning masquerade. Their chief vocation is to strengthen 'the Law,'

45

uphold 'the Constitution,' vote the annual 'Appropriations' and devise ways and means of exploiting the nation or of permitting it to be systematically looted by their accomplices, or—their Masters.

The principles that govern a 'hold-up' are the self-same principles that govern government. No government on earth rests on the consent of the governed.

Is it reasonable therefore for a confederation of masterful bandits to place themselves in positions of absolute equality, before their intended victims? The idea is absurd on the face of it. Brigandage necessitates inequality: and every government on earth, is organized and enthroned Brigandage.*

Las Casas, the Spanish Jesuit, was the first American to spread about the false, subversive, and shameful theory of 'equal human rights' but since his time, it has been boastfully accepted on all sides, by vast hordes of witless persons who are in all countries, the numerical majority. "The race of fools" as Plato sagaciously remarked, "is not to be counted "—not even in this—"land of the free."

Although Equality (in any shape) has never been scientifically proven nor logically defended, nevertheless it passes from tongue to tongue, from brain to brain in current discussions, for 'gospel truth'—just as clever counterfeit coins are passed unsuspectingly from hand to hand.

The Equality superstition is tolerated by clear-seeing men, for one reason only. It assists them to govern the thoughts: and by governing the thoughts, to exploit the property, energy, and labor-force, of their soft-minded good-natured neighbors: who really believe it to be true—who think it, glad tidings of Great Joy.

Behold! when the fraudulent 'equality of natural rights' evangel, is mellifluously poured forth in the Market Places by suave dollar-hunting attorneys, or half-educated mechanics, even those staid citizens (whose whole life is of it a direct disproof) lead the roaring, raving, yelling crowd, in its maniacal bellowings.

Lo! the Angel of Lunacy is camped in their souls!

🜲 8 🜲

Every atom of organic matter has its own vital peculiarity. Every animate being is different in osseous structure and chemical composition. Ethnology, Biology, History, all proclaim Equality to be a myth. Even the great epics of antiquity are all glorifications of

---

* "Have we not shown that Government is essentially immoral?"— *Herbert Spencer*

46

inequality: inequality of mind—inequality of birth, of courage or condition. Can equality of body, equality of mind, equality of origin, equality before the law, or any other kind of 'equality' be demonstrated by any one fact?

Mentally and morally, every breathing being is a self poised monad—a differentiated ego. No two germs, planets, suns or stars, are alike. Among the higher vertebrates this is especially so, and consequently, the only law that men ought to honor or respect, is the law that originates, and finds its sanction *in themselves*—in their own consciousness.

Inequality is summed up in the scientific axiom "inferior organisms succumb, that superior organisms may survive, propogate, and possess." In other words, the proper place for Lazarus is to rot among the dogs. And the proper place for Ceaser is at the head of his irresistible legions.

From the soles of his feet to the crown of his head—the bones, skin and flesh of his body—even the gray brain pulp—the electric nerves and tissues—mental ganglia and internal viscera of a man belonging to the African, Mongolian, Semite, or Negrito breeds are all fundamentally different in formation, constituents and character, from the corresponding anatomical section of men of Aryan descent. The points of non-resemblance may be superficially imperceivable, but they are organic—deep seated.

Notwithstanding the dexterous writers of strategic fables, dross is dross, gold is gold, and some men *are* born better, born nobler, born braver than others.

Aristocracy by birth rests upon an unalterable scientific basis of heredity and selection; but an aristocracy of money rests mainly upon bolts and bars; i.e., upon laws, that may be abrogated at a moment's notice.

Though unable to reason out, in logical sequence their inherent abhorrence of social and racial equality yet most men instinctively detest it—in practice.

What white father, for example, would encourage the marriage of a hulking thick-skulled Negro with his beautiful and accomplished daughter? Would he enthusiastically 'give her away' to the matrimonial embraces of a Chinaman, a Coolie, or the leper-hugs of a polluted 'mean white?' Are there ten such citizens even in North America, where equality of birth and condition is so much speechified and—*never* seen? Are there five? Is there one who would not rather see the daughter of his loins, stiff, stark, and cold in her shroud? Should that *one* exist (he being of sound mind) let him speak. Then and only then, can this diabolical gospel of intrinsic equality be reconsidered.

Meanwhile, plain practical citizens are justified in regarding it, not as a self-evident truth, but an insolent, malignant, and abominable lie—a lie that shall yet be stamped out forever—with blood and fire.

You have only to look at some men, to know that they belong to an inferior breed. Take the Negro, for example. His narrow cranial development, his prognathous jaw, his projecting lips, his wide nasal aperture, his simian disposition, his want of forethought, originality, and mental capacity, are all peculiarities strictly inferior. Similar language may be applied to the Chinaman, the Coolie, the Kanaka, the Jew, and to the rotten-boned city degenerates of Anglo-Saxondom: rich and poor. Vile indeed are the inhabitants of those noxious cattle kraals: London, Liverpool, New York, Chicago, New Orleans; and yet, in those places is heaped up the golden plunder of the world.

Ethnographists of the very highest authority, assert that over ten thousand years ago, the black, white, and yellow types of men-animals were as pronounced, and as ineffaceable as they are to-day. The hieroglyphics and records of ancient tombs and monuments, cuneiform inscriptions, antiquarian researches, and the systematic study of pre-historic skulls and skeletons all bear the same uniform testimony.

Inequality of birth and condition, can never perish from off the earth. Never! and why should it? Who can fill the valleys up and lay the mountains low?

🐦 9 🐦

Even the giddy doctrinaire who so cunningly concocted the bombastes-furioso fictions of the Declaration* could not apparently have believed them himself. Was he not a slave-driver (residing among slave-drivers) who bought and auctioned human cattle for dollars and cents *all the days of his life?* No doubt for purposes of state-craft and necessary war-craft he wove his philosophic preamble of Strong Deceit. Probably also, he was comparatively honest, and even sincere but among the alluring priests of Unreason, the most dangerous is the fanatical propagandist.

When Jefferson dictated his fatal and untenable abstractions, he was not even original but plagiarized Zeno the Stoic, Jack

---

* Mayhap, Franklin (who had a comic vein), wrote them as grinning jokes. By the way, every signature attached thereto represents a slave-holding, slave-trading constituency. All the colonies traded in niggers.

Cade, Savonarola, Milton, Plate, John Ball, etc. Zeno said: "All men are by nature equal," but carefully refrained from attempting to demonstrate it. Milton defended it in his prose essays, Plato voiced it in his *Republic*, John Ball preached it in medieval England, Savonarola perished trying to establish it in Florence. Jack Cade, Robespierre and Christ were also failures—ghastly failures.

"If human experience proves anything at all," writes James Fitzjames Stephens, "it proves, that if the restraints are minimized, if the largest possible measure of Liberty is accorded to all human beings; the result will not be equality but inequality, reproducing itself in a geometrical ration." Remove the restraints and see how quickly an aristocracy based on Merit would mow down an aristocracy based on Credit.

In actual life, he who claims equality with another, is ever called upon to prove his claim, not by a grotesque abracadabra of silly phrases, parroted from antique philosophers or blue-mouldy documents but by actual deeds—that is to say, by producing his credentials. Constitutional theories are all very well to humbug stridulating slaves but in a freeman's household, or business, they are not 'legal tender.' Among men of affairs, natural egalitarianism, is regarded as amusing moonshine—mere spread-eagleism, fit for public meetings only. Business minds thoroughly understand (having learnt by bitter experience), that some men are destined by Nature to bear command and some to obey: aye, even for a thousand years before their birth.

No one can study the laborers on a farm, the 'hands' in a big foundry or factory, the seamen in a large seaport, the nomadic hirelings on a railroad construction gang, or the clerks and salesmen in a city warehouse, without perceiving at a glance, that the vast majority of them are extremely poor specimens of humanity.

The ideal type of manhood or womanhood (that is to say, 'Ye Thoroughbred'), is not to be found among these captive hordes— for captives they really are. Their heads are to a large extent unsymmetrical, their features distorted, ape-like, unintelligent. Their bodies are out of all proportion, dwarfed, stunted, diseased, malformed, cretinous.

Their movements are contracted, artificial, ungainly, and their minds (outside of routine) are utter vacuums. When compared with the traditional ideal of Strength, Beauty, Courage and Nobleness of character, they are an extremely ill-bred herd of cattle, exhibiting all the psychological stigmata of inherited brain-rot and of physical decay. "A crown of thorns on every brow—that IS the wage they're earning now."*

* Ibsen.

Nine-tenths of them are positively repulsive in language, mentality, and in general appearance. They even display an extraordinarily low average of animality, and upon the slightest exposure perish off, like sheep that have the lung worm. Heated rooms, woolen clothing, and stimulating beverages, are the means whereby their watery blood is kept in languid circulation. Every new generation is feebler, and more debased than its predecessor. All the scientific evidences of mental, moral, and bodily deterioration, are markedly accentuated in them and—their timidity is proverbial.*

Hard, continuous, methodical labor, destroys courage, saps vitality, and demoralizes character. It tames and subdues men, just as it tames and subdues the wild steer or the young colt. Men who labor hard and continuously have no power to think. It requires all their vital force to keep their muscles in trim.

Indeed, the civilized city working-man and working-woman are the lowest and worst type of animal ever evolved from dust and slime and oxygen. They actually worship Work, and bow down before Law as an ox-team crouches and strains under the lash.

Look upon their shrunken cheeks, their thin lips, their narrow retreating irresolute jaws, their decayed teeth, sharp puny noses, small watery eyes, yellow bloodless complexions, bent shoulders, dry hair tending to baldness, struggling thin beard; the woman with pinched features, waspish fragile waists, want of bust development, consumptive, neurotic, artificially barren, emaciated, hungry, dwarfed, hysterical.

The minds of average workmen and workwomen, are either total vacuums or stuffed to the brim with every conceivable species of lies, iniquity, superstition, and sham. Indeed how could they remain in such conditions of base, loathsome hirelingism, were they not deficient in all the Primitive Virtues—in all that is manly and womanly?

Behold!—upon their brow is stamped (with red-hot cattle brands) the word "DAMNED." Eternally tortured are they in a patent purgatory invented by Politicians. Their tribulations however may really be but Progression in disguise, because their shameful self-degradation must ultimately end in their utter extinguishment. Hopelessly are they entangled in the snare—hopelessly defeated. For them there is no escape—No! not even through fields of blood.

Poor trembling wretches!—washing their own hands in their own sweat!—nay, in their own heart's blood! Born thralls are they—or, born madmen!

---

* "The brave man may fail sometimes, but the coward fails always."—*Angelo Mosso*

Their days are without hope, and their years are consumed for—naught. When their Masters speak unto them, there is trembling in all their joints.

They waste their lives pursuing shadows, and for hire, build their own tombs. Their minds are below freezing point, nay! below zero! Crippled souls are they.

They knead their own flesh into daily bread, and transmute their 'contrite hearts' into basins of gruel.

They look unto *Idols* for deliverance,* aye and grind their dry bones into baskets of coal. At thoughts of battle they blanch with terror; at sight of naked bayonets, they run like whipped hounds.

Therefore Strength leapeth down upon them as the panther leaps upon his quarry. And in a moment of time they are blotted out.

My soul abhorreth them as an abomination. My hand reacheth out to clutch them by the throat.

Heredity has ever so much more to do with social conditions than the majority of modern men are willing to admit, judging by results that nations ignore Birth and Breeding at their peril for just as there are noble animals, there are noble-men. If a stock-raiser throws down his dividing fences and permits *all* his cattle to mix-up promiscuously together: what kind of a herd would he have, say, in one decade? Nothings but weeds, hybrids and mongrels!

Now, that is exactly what nations attempt when they endeavor to establish an equality of privileges and of happy, peaceful conditions.

The close psychological connection that exists between ancestry and degeneracy, crime, genius, insanity, etc., etc., is now everywhere being acknowledged, thanks to the researches of Galton, Lombroso, Mosso, Otto Ammon, Ferri, Kraft Ebbing, and others.

If criminals are criminals, by descent, or by birth, is it not equally probable that slaves are slaves by the facts of their breed and ancestry? Does it not also follow that heros and strong, powerful, resolute personalities have derived their solid stamina from their forefathers? Indeed, all history and all geneologies

---

* When the Roman Empire was tottering to its fall, the worship of the State was an established cult: just as it is to-day. Better to adore blocks of wood or stone, than bow our hearts, our heads and our knees, before those troops of Unclean Beasts—Politicians!

prove that this is a mathematical fact. Great men are ever the descendants of mighty warriors and conquerers: that is to say, of mighty animals.

Von Otto Ammon cites a remarkable instance, which goes to prove the selective and ethnic advantages of Warfare. He states that all German children born during the Franco-Prussian campaign of '71 (also the years immediately following) show a strikingly high average excellence, both of body and mind.

The converse is equally demonstrable. Show me a herd of humans who have been underfed day-drudges from their youth up and I will show you a herd of cattle whose ancestors were also propertyless vassals and serfs, beaten in diplomacy and in war for ages past. (Take the Irish peasantry and the fellaheen of Egypt as examples.) This statement admits of no qualification, for if one exception can be discovered, it will serve to prove the general rule. A *man* in the full possession of all his faculties, of leonine ancestry, well born, self-contained, would rather cut his own throat from ear to ear, with a blacksmith's rasp, than live the life of an average hired laborer in any civilized "hell" on earth.

The nexus between self-mastership and breed is of tremendous significance. Therein is the Lost Secret.

Undoubtedly new born infants *are* daily coming wailing into this world, with the words—statesman, tramp, wastrel, warrior, priest, philosopher, criminal, thief, king, slave and coward, indelibly branded upon their brows, their hearts and their brains.

Our talents, our virtues and our vices, depend entirely upon our individual mechanism; and that mechanism is the result of countless chemical transformations, extending over ages but modified to a large extent by climate and soil. "What is bred in the bone, will never come out of the flesh," wrote Pilpay thousands of years ago. There is a pregnant ethnic philosophy in four lines (quoted from Keramos):

"This clay well mixed with marl and sand,
Follows the motion of my hand;
For some must follow, and some command:
Though all are made of clay."

Although *all* may be made of clay in the poetic sense, it must never be forgotten that the clay itself is composed of differentiated elements. The clay that is in a Blackfellow or a Chinaman, is not the clay that is in a Shakespeare or a Bismarck. Some "clay" will grow good wheat and make very bad bricks, just as some breeds of animals are born to be hunters and others born to be hunted. Some clay will raise splendid crops, even from poor seed; and some never produces anything (no matter how highly cultivated) except thorns and weeds and nettles and poisons. The natures of men are moulded almost entirely by the nature of the soil from which they have been grown. Man is a perambulating crop. In some places he grows to perfection; in other localities he won't grow at all or runs to seed. In India, the Anglo Saxon dwindles and dwindles, but in Canada and the Northern States he even develops increased stamina.

All science, all history, and all experience are unanimous in disproof of equal natural rights for *all* men (that strident doctrine of the fool); and yet the insolent, proofless assertions of a Zeno, a Jefferson, a Jack Cade, Robespierre, or a Jewish Carpenter (when fantastically engrossed and framed or bound in a book) are passively accepted by the intellectual serfs of this degenerate nineteenth century, and trumpeted to the ends of the earth as a sublime and holy revelation. Equalitaryism passes almost unchallenged in public orations, because to openly question its veracity, is felt to be unpopular; and with the noble leaders of public opinion in all democracies, popularity is everything—the alpha and the omega, the beginning and the end. The result in Anglo-Saxondom is simply nauseous.

Young men are mentally mutilated, systematically "educated" by schools, press and literature, upon fundamental hallucinations, pyrotechnic shams, and glittering illusions— illusions that are the perennial source of fruitless servile uprisings, social heart-burnings, internecine unpleasantnesses and sundry other secondary symptoms of social cancer.

Our Government Educational Systems are absolutely under the direct control of Politicians. These Priests-of-the-State select and train the teachers, vote salaries and dictate what Truths and Lies the textbooks shall contain. Indeed our National Schools are managed upon the same jesuitic plan, whereby the monks and prelates of old, successfully worked the Universal Church. "Come right in here and we'll improve your minds free of cost," suavely saith the high priests of this New Idolatry—this devouring Dragon—this Impersonal State. So the pure-hearted rosy-cheeked little ones enter unsuspectingly. Gradually as they are "brought under the influence" the gray brain-pulp is forced out of plastic young skulls, and lies, nice pretty poetic lies (mixed with unavoidable facts and perverted truths) skillfully injected. Did you ever see medical students extract the brain of a frog and then fill up the vacuum with pith? The frog does not die, it lives, hops about quite lively, and seems to possess its former intelligence and vitality, but it is all illusion. What experimental vivisectionists do to frogs, state-priests do to the children of men.

Bit by bit, with dates and lists and emasculated histories, the iniquitous brain-wrecking deviltry proceeds. When completed, young men and women are turned out with addled brains, into a warring world, incapables, semi-imbiciles, unable to defend or assert themselves—footballs of fate, ready to *serve* anyone. Is it not notorious, the ineptitude, mechanical imitativeness, and want of initiative, displayed by state-educated young men? Instead of being urged to *think* and *act* for themselves, they are taught, like well-drilled slaves to Believe and Obey. They are even trained to glorify and worship Idols, with strident shouts and modulated canticles—not honest Idols of wood and stone, but Idols of sheepskin, bound pamphlets, variegated rags and the falsified Renown of dead Scoundrels, i.e., Statesmen.

It requires a stout rope, a firm post and muscular men to hold an *unbroken* colt; but when by Force and petting he has once been subdued, i.e., tamed, educated, saddled, bridled, he may be led anywhere even with a piece of twine in the hands of a little child. O, ye State-Priests, so adroit, so eloquent! Ye cunning demons! Ye wolves in sheep's clothing! Ye corrupters of Youth! Ye generation of vipers! How can you escape from the wrath to come? How can you escape *someday* from being "hung up, by the tongue on the red-hot hooks, of a real live hell."

Thirty years ago the United States quixotically essayed to demonstrate racial equality with rifle bullets and bomb-shells; but failed most ignominiously. Southern valleys were strewn with Northern and Southern bones and millions of tax-treasure blown from the lips of cannon without any tangible result, except to demonstrate before an interested world, the utter failure and hollowness of equality principles.

A people that deliberately enters upon a gigantic war in order to firmly establish a Centralized Despotism; and at the same time reduce itself to the social level of the Negro, the Russian Jew, the Coolie, the Chinaman, and the European Serf, must indeed (to use a suggestive vernacularism) have "wheels in its head."

The "man and brother" lie has certainly succeeded in writing itself in a "constitutional amendment." but in real life it is as far from actuality as ever it was. The "free" Negro of New Orleans or Charleston is a more degraded, more despised being; and of less money value to his proprietors now than when it was customary to buy and sell him at the auction block, instead of as at present on the Stock Exchange.

What the late civil war really accomplished, was to degrade the white slave to the lower level of the plantation nigger, and in that respect it was a triumph of ingenuity. The Whites fought—actually fought each other to demonetize themselves. Equality! Equality! what brilliant deeds have been "perpetrated" in thy name? Lincoln however! was he not "a great statesman?"

Decidedly he was! Well indeed *he* knew how to 'round-up' the herd with bewitching phrases!

Hark! do you hear those drunken slaves caterwauling down the street? Lo! it is election night! "Hurrah! hurrah!" they sing, "We'll sound the jubilee! Glory be to Lincoln, the man who made *us* free." In Morocco the eunuchs and other menials, bless their fate and the Prince, at the very time he condescends to cut *their* throats with *his* own hands. Americans, however, are a free-born people not to be duped that way.

Throughout both Northern and Southern states, the social chasm between the highest and lowest human organisms (whether white or black, or black-and-tan), is even more pronounced now, than ever it was previously. For example, although Negroes are a majority in many States, they are never permitted to attain actual administrative power and they never shall.

You cannot paint the Negro white, with laws and constitutions: though you write it in the fire and smoke of wars and revolutions.

To solemnly proclaim that "all men are created equal," is as stupid and unscientific as to assert that all dogs, cattle, apes and trees are created equal.

Is there not as many diverse varieties of dogs, cattle, apes and trees as there are of men, planets, germs, stars and suns? Where then is the intrinsic equality between an oak tree and a currant bush—between a mettlesome wolf-hound and a yelping street cur—between a buffalo bull and a hand-fed steer—between an untameable gorilla of the woods and an organ-grinder's castrated monkey—between a cosmic-brained Bismarck and that famous Christling, "the good young man that died?" Cannot a blooded bulldog whip a solid score of lean, half-starved street mongrels? Upon exactly the same principle, a small body of bold, self-reliant brainy men are ever more a match (under any circumstances), for 10,000, nay, 10,000,000 greasy mechanics. What is a mechanic anyhow but a specially trained slave?—and it would take the spirit of 1,000 American slaves to make that of one live man. Theoretically, all these organisms are of "the same species," but in the savage rush for bread, love, space and life, there are as many functional differences between them as there are between a royal Bengal tiger and "Mary's little lamb." The lamb was made to be eaten and the tiger was made to eat it; and man was born to struggle as the sparks fly upwards.

The necessities of environment make of each man, the enemy or rival of other men, more especially, those with whom he comes in direct personal conflict. Where then does equality come in? It does not 'come in' at all. It is an idiotic myth. There must always be a substratum of victimized organisms. How could the tiger live if there were no lambs to devour? How could there be heroes if there were no slaves? How could there be great nations if there were no contemptible ones?

Compare the noble qualities inherent in some dogs with the obsequious "virtues" that distinguish nine men out of ten. Now, give to canine or homo equal liberty of action—equal opportunity—equal "rights," and what will be the result? Must not the fiercest fighter fatten, while the skeletons of lean weaklings project through their scrofulous hides? What power *origninating among themselves* could dictate and enforce—equality of opportunity?

Socialism, Christianism, Democratism, Equalityism, are really the whining yelps of base-bred mongrel-multitudes. They howl aloud for State intervention—"protection for suffering humanity"—regulated mill-grinding as it were; with the State to be their Supreme Idol, their God and Master, their All in All, their Great Panjandrum. Poor deluded base spirited "weeds." Truly the "Curse of God" is in the very marrow of their bones—in every pump-stroke of their dying hearts.

The man who prays to be "protected" by politicians, guarded by armed Janissaries, saved by idolatrous priests, and redeemed by State Regimentation is indeed a miserable sinner—a vile, despicable, un-manly wretch.

🐉12🐉

No paternalistic governmental mechanism (however theoretically perfect), can ever keep the base-born and the well-born, the thoroughbreds and the hybrids, in a state of perpetual equilibrium. You might as well try to bind down an earthquake with hoop-iron, as to rule the Strong with "be it enacted." "Be it enacteds" were invented only to frighten captives with.

What power on earth can permanently keep the Negro on a parity with the Anglo-Saxon?

The Strong must have their way in spite of all puritanic proscribings, all mock moralisms, all degrading legalisms, all constitutional covenantings. Neither the machinery nor the raw material of equality has ever existed; only the dream, the idea of it. Equality! Equality! in that one word is summed up the accumulated dementia of two thousand years! The thought of it was born in the brain of an inferior organism: and the brains of inferior organisms nourish it still.

How can beings who for ages have been born and bred to toil and subjectivity, ever comprehend the feelings of those who are free-born, and of valorous descent—of those who understand the cosmic law that Might is—Master?

You cannot muzzle a tempest with a cobweb, bridle a volcano with a shoe-string, bottle up a cyclone in a powder horn, nor catch a tidal wave with a boat-hook. Neither can you put a bit between the teeth of the Strong. They will see you—in Sheol first.

No artificial plan of society—no pious incantations however sincere and well intentioned; can ever prevent the pot that is of iron from smashing and sinking the pot that is of clay—and why should it? If social equilibrium had been feasible, it would have been established ages and ages ago. It never has been established—and it never shall.*

What then is the good of eternally dreaming, theorizing, and constructing phantom castles-in-the-air, cities of god, and gardens of delight, upon foundations of deliberate unveracity? Let us be men—whole men—not clamorous, tearful little children demanding infantile sugar-plums. Let us face the fierce challenging *facts* of existence as boldly as our forefathers did before "Christly comfort and consolation" was introduced to un-man them—not like crouching, cringing, terrorized, oriental pariahs. Let us not be lured to wholesale annihilation by sonorous Asiatic evangelisms, that have proven themselves worthless and unsuitable to our temperament, our climate, and our breed. Let us be sensible, brave, practical; and as Virchow somewhat trenchantly recommends: *"accept things as they really are, not as we choose to imagine them"*—or rather as they have been imagined by dotard philosophers, daft poets, and castrated clerics.

 13

The problem that we are ever called upon to solve or be eaten up, is not how to make life 'happy and equal' for happiness is a moving mirage, and equality an impossibility, but how men may conquer their Opportunities, surpass their Rivals, extirpate their Pursuers.

The race is still to the swift and the battle to the strong. Beauty

---

* "Man has a right to subsitence," wrote Thomas Paine. "Yes," replied an observant reader, "he has a right to live one thousand years, *if he can*." It is not a problem of Right but of Ability—Strength.

and booty are always the prerogatives of victorious valor. Woe to the outgeneralled ones!

"'Tis a battle for bread, for love, and for breath,
'Tis a race for life to the jaws of death."*

Upon the island of Java there is a remarkable valley of death. It is literally strewn with the bones and skulls and skeletons of innumerable dead animals and creeping things. In the due season, giant turtles, five foot by three in diameter, travel up through it from the sea, to lay their eggs. En-route, they are set upon by packs of wild dogs and these dogs roll the turtles over upon their backs and then devour them alive, by tearing out their unprotected entrails. When the dogs are gorged, they in their turn, fall an easy prey to ambushed tigers. Then hunters kill these tigers for their variegated skins. Rank grass springs up after the rainy season, through the skulls and bones that litter this tropical golgotha and droves of cattle gather there to fatten. Again, the cattle are hunted for their hides, horns, and flesh, and their bones are also left where they fall, to manure the valley and prepare it for new generations of hunters and hunted. Such is in miniature, a picture of the every-day world as it actually is. All living beings are pursuing and—being pursued. Woe unto those that stumble! Woe unto Ye who fall!

They who accept the "Equality, Faith, Hope, and Charity" ideal, in any shape or form whatever, interpret the facts of mortal life as they are not—as they have never been, as they can never be. Indeed when the animal world becomes 'moralized' and 'equalized' it will be extinct. No doubt when contemplating the dark side of all this, Pascal was impelled to write with superstitious medieval diapasson: 'I am affrighted like a man who in his sleep has been carried unto some horrible desert island, and there awakes not knowing where he is, nor how he shall escape.'

Degenerates only are thus affrighted at the tragic majesty of their surroundings.

If this struggle is ordained of us, why not enter into it with kindly courage, with dauntless delight? Why not go forward, daring all things, to conquer or to die?

Is it not better to perish than to serve? "Liberty or death" is *not* a meaningless phrase. No! it is of tremendous import to those who—comprehend.

What is death that it should make cowards of us all? What is life that it should be valued so highly? There are worse things than death and among them is a life of dishonor. All men lead dishonorable lives who serve a master with hand or brain.

* *P. Luftig*—"Bulletin," Australia.

Life itself is but a spark in the gloom that flashes out and disappears. Why therefore not make the most of it here and now—Here and Now!

There is no "heaven of glory bright," and no hell where sinners roast. There is no Right, there is no Wrong—nor God—nor Son—nor Ghost.

Death endeth all for every man,
For every "son of thunder":
Then be a Lion in the path;
And don't be trampled under.

For us there is no rest—no Kingdom of Indolence, either on this earth or beyond the skies—no Isles of the Blest—no Elysian Fields—no garden of the Hesperides. No! No! All these magical legends are but fanciful waking dreams—"fiction of mortals of yore."

Here and *now* is our day of torment! Here and *now* is our day of joy! Here and *now* is our Opportunity—to eat or be eaten—to be Lion or Lamb! Here and *now* it is war to the knife—no escape—no retreat. Choose ye this day, this hour, for no Redeemer liveth!

Every attempt made to organize the Future must necessarily collapse. The Present is our Domain and our chief duty is to take immediate possession thereof upon strict business principles.

Strive therefore against them that strive against you, and war against them that war against thine. Lay hold of shield and buckler or their equivalents, stand up! Be a Terrible one in thine own defense. Raise up also the Clenched Hand and stop the way of them that would persecute you. Say unto thine own heart and soul "I, even I, am my own redeemer."

Let them be hurled back to confusion and infamy, who devise thine undoing. Let them be as chaff before the cyclone and let the Angel of Death pursue them, nay overtake them. In a pit, they have hidden a trap for *thy* feet: into that very destruction let them fall. Then, exultant, "sound the loud timbrel." Rejoice! Rejoice! in thine own salvation. Then all thy bones shall say pridefully "who is like unto me?"—Have I not delivered myself by mine own brain? Have I not been too strong for mine adversaries?—Have I not spoiled them that would have spoiled me?

14

This circling planet-ball is no navel-contemplating Nirvana, but rather a vast whirling star-lit Valhalla, where victorious battlers quaff the foaming hearts-blood of their smashed-up adversaries, from the scooped out skull goblets of the slain in neverending war.

And behold it is good! It is good! It is very good!
"Blending in bloody strife,
Throat to throat, life for life;
Struggles the human still."
And in that invigorating struggle strength is renewable. Fitness to reign, propogate and possess, can there alone be tested with mathematical precision (in nature's majestic Judgment Hall), that is to say on the plains of Conquest where foeman looks into foeman's eye and death lurks, like a ravenous leopard, in every bush.

Those who claim mastership on any other basis than Conquest are Upstarts, Usurpers, and ought therefore to be deposed without pity, and without mercy in accordance with the cosmic decree of ethnic displacement. Death I say!—Death!

Life is a duel and only the Fittest can possibly hope to succeed. If you would Survive O reader! (in the highest meaning of that word) go to, and put some splendor in your deeds. Beware of false philosophies that equalize *you* with slavelings and dastards! Beware of fattened priestlings and tax-collecting statesmen!

Beware the tongue that is smoothly hung, and never forget for one moment, that your greatest enemies upon earth are those crafty courtiers who eloquently, cunningly flatter you, that they may first win your heart, and then—skin you alive. The modern Mephistopheles is the soft-toned preacher in his pulpit—the editorial sophist in his net-work of lies—the political crocodile on his "planks" and his "platforms."

A trinity of hell-hounds are they! Oh! Would that they had but one neck and I was—Judge Lynch!

America! America! in spite of all the surreptitious bonds that in thy sleep have been laid upon thee yet pregnant thy womb is with men of Nerve—men of Valor—men of Might. Lo! the hour approacheth when in dire travail thou shalt give birth unto Thunderbolts, and Joves to handle them.

Behold that time cometh! Nay, it is at hand! But it will not be a period of pure delight. No! No!—it will be a day of wrath, a dreadful day—a day of Judgement, Tribulation, Triumph.

And Democracy! Democracy! thou leprous thing!—thou loathsome disease!—thou plastic demon!—thou murderer of man! Many nations have bowed down to thy infection, and perished from off the earth, but America! America! shall wipe thee out—thou blightsome malady—thou human rinderpest!

Verily! Verily! a new nobility shall be born unto thee O America!—a breed of Terrible Commanders !—of Grim Destroyers—A nobility unpurchaseable with the minted tokens of money-changers—a nobility of Valor, of Power and Might—a nobility honorable, clear-sighted, clean-skinned, *unconquerable.*

Through the Future shines the sun of splendid struggle. Heroic Natures there lead us on, as they led at Illion. The Natural Man steps forth once more in all his daring grandeur, Smashing unclean Idols, defying Gods and Laws and slave-made Morals.

 15

THE PHILOSOPHY OF POWER
(Condensed)

How did government of man by man originate?
By force of arms. Victors became rulers.
But among *us* government by force is abolished?
That is a popular delusion. It is stronger than ever.
How is it that we do not see it clearly?
No need of compulsion with inferiors ever eager to obey.
How can the Mastership of man be destroyed?
It can never be destroyed. It is essential.
But for one man to reign over another is wrong?
What is 'wrong'? The Strong can do as they please.
Who are the 'Strong'?
They who conquer. They who take the spoil and camp on the battlefield. All life is a battlefield.
How did subjectiveness originate?
The first slave was a defeated fighter, afterwards tamed by hunger and blows. His descendants being born and trained to submissiveness are more tractable. All the Servile Classes are posterity of beaten battlers.
Then vassalage still flourishes as of yore?
Certainly. In the pitiless strife for existence, all weaklings and feeble-minded persons are justly subordinated.
But we are taught 'all men are created equal'?
You are taught many a diplomatic Lie.
How can a slave recover his liberty?
By re-conquering his conquerer. If he feels that he is not man enough then he *must* submit, cut his own throat, or die fighting unsubdued.
But freedom may be granted to him?
'Freedom can not be granted, it must be taken.'
Then Strife is perpetual, inevitable, nay, glorious?
Yes! It is intended as an ordeal, a trial by combat. It unmistakably

61

divides the guilty from the non-guilty.

But that is a harsh philosophy?

Nature is harsh, cruel, merciless to all unlovely things. Her smile is only for the Courageous, the Strong, the Beautiful and the All-Daring.

You have no comfort for the 'poor and lowly,' the 'innocent ones,' the 'downtrodden'?

The poor and the lowly are creeping pestilence—there are no innocent ones, and the downtrodden are the justly damned—sinners in a hell they've made.

You praise the Strong, you glorify the Mighty Ones?

I do. They are Nature's noblemen. In them she delights: the All-Vanquishers! the Dauntless Ones!

𝕏 4 𝕏

MAN — THE CARNIVORE!

It has taken countless evolutionary epochs to make man what he is: the most ferocious hirstute beast of prey that inhabits the caverns and jungles of earth.

Can his osseous mechanism and pathological instincts be summarily extinguished or reversed, merely by connecting him, per an electric wire, laid through the sewers of Rome, to the feeble dynamos of Bethlehem and Tarsus? Can his structural anatomy, intended for conflict and slaughter, be transformed in a day, a year, or even "a million, million of suns?"

To overmaster and devour his neighbor, in the reasoned effort to obtain food and booty, land, love, renown and gold is bred into the very marrow of his bones. Therefore, all efforts made by Reformers and Messiahs, to transfigure him into a "lamb" are foreordained to fathomless failure. Indeed it would be much more reasonable of them to attempt the transformation of a grizzly bear into a parlor poodle or propose the transformation of a bald-headed eagle into a gently cooing turtle-dove.

Nearly all the prophetic demi-gods of Democracy from Paul and Isaiah to Carlyle and Ruskin, have ever been madly screeching by the roadside, vainly endeavoring to stay the march! march! march! of a world of bannered armies; striding grimly, sternly by. What are these howling prophets of Evil but dogs eloquently baying at the moon? "Right wheel there! Right wheel! Turn back! Turn back! You are going to the devil!" is their resounding ear-splitting chorus. But the human flood sweeps on silently, scornfully, confident, inspired as it were by some over-mastering instinct. "We may be going to the devil," is the unspoken retort of these thundering legionaires—these Nations "but even so! is not the Devil honest—the Destroyer of Deception!—the Disobedient One?"

Can you lasso the stars with a green-hide lariat? Can you block the march of Might with magnificent howls of declamatory

63

despair? No! No! Skyward or hellward, man moves on and on and on. If there are barricades in his way, he must surmount them or blast them aside. If there are Wild Beasts ready to spring upon him, he must destroy them or they will destroy him. If the highroad leads through hells, then those infernos must be besieged, assailed and taken possession of—aye, even if their present monarchs have to be rooted-out with weapons as demonic and deadly as their own.

This world is too peaceful, too acquiescent, too tame. It is a circumcised world. Nay!—a castrated world! It must be made fiercer, before it can become grander and better and—more natural.

Fools indeed are they who would arrest the unfolding process with "humanitarian" Cagliostroism, and "rescue the perishing" mummery. Maniacs are they who would ward off the sun's blazing rays from withering souls or the blighted frosts of winter from hearts that are already broken. For, I doubt not, through the ages, one tremendous purpose runs; and maturing crops are ripened with the process of the suns—to be sickled down, threshed and rolled away.

❈ 2 ❈

Undoubtedly the Black Magic of the Christ Myth, combined with the subterranean sorcery of medieval sacredotalism *has* partially succeeded, not only in sapping individual initiative, but also in suppressing in our Race many of its ancestral leonine traits and superb Barbarian Virtues. But as yet, it has not wholly triumphed in its emasculating necromancy. No! it has not transfigured *us all* into teams of contented oxen and bunches of earmarked sheep, although that is its final hope. There *are some* of the grand old stock, left alive. Few indeed are they amidst a world of slaves and swine.

The lion is still the lion, although his teeth have been most foully filed down by abominable moral codes; his skin made scrofulous with the mange and leprosy of caged peacefulness—his paws fettered by links of slave-voted statutes and an iron collar of State Officialism wound around his regal neck.

Someday, sometime he is destined to break through the vile bonds that have been cunningly laid on him, escape from the wasting decline that originates from unnatural confinement and regain once more his primitive freedom of Action. The treacherous legislators and illustrious statesmen, who are now so eager to teach him the method of growing wool like sheep and how to fit his battle-scarred shoulders to a horse collar, may then be sorry and sad (if they have time)—for he will probably chew them up.

Great and powerful governments, Commanding Peace, come into existence *only* in ages of decadence; when nations are on the downward grade. If the human animal lives a natural, cleanly life, out on the plains and forests, away where ocean rollers crash along the shore, or on the banks of the pouring rivers, he requires no police-force to "protect" him—no usurous Jews to rob him of his harvests—no tax-gathering legislators to vote away his property, and no 'priests of the Idol' to "save" his soul.

It is false standards of morality that debase and enfeeble individuals, tribes and nations. First, in obedience to some sovereign code, they lose their hardihood and increase their numbers. Then that *all* may live, they become laborious, submissive to Regulations; and finally—with Death held up by priest-craft as a fearsome Terror, all personal valor fades away. Thus nations of spaniels are manufactured.

The normal man is the man that loves and feasts and fights and hunts—the predatory man. The abnormal man is he that toils for a master, half-starves, and "thinks"—the Christly dog. The first is a perfect animal; the second, a perfect—monster.

Every belief that makes a duty of humility—that inspires a people with "moral" courage only, enervates their fibre, corrupts their spirit, and prepares them first for thraldom and then for—throttling.

It is not possible to conceive of Grand Life without incessant rivalry, perpetual warfare and the implacable hunting of man by man.

Terror, torture, agony and the wholesale destruction of feeble and worn out types, must mark in future, as in the past, every step forward, or backward in evolution, homo-culture and racial displacement.

The soil of every nation is an arena, a stamping ground, where only the most vigorous *animals* may hope to hold their own. What is all history but the epic of a colossal campaign, the final Armageddon of which is never likely to be fought, because, when men cease to fight—they cease to be—Men.

This old earth is strewn to the very mountain-tops with the fleshless skulls and rain bleached bones of perished combatants in countless myriads. Every square foot, every inch, of soil contains its man.

3

The evolution (or de-evolution) of mankind demands the perpetual transfiguration of one man into another, continuous reincarnation, eternal re-birth and re-construction. Scientifically considered, the "resurrection of the dead" is not an illusion. Every living organism is formed from the decomposed essence of pre-existent organisms. The "man" of to-day is actually built out of the grave-mold of his prototypes, perhaps of ages long forgotten. Thus, without death there could be no birth-material; and without conflict, fierce and deadly, there could be no surpassing.

But to individuals foolishly trained to bewail their fate, all these commonplace facts are agonizing.

"When we solemnly look upon this perpetual conflict," writes Schelling with true theocratic pessimism, "it fills us with shuddering sorrow, and with boundless alarm—but how can we help it? Hence the veil of sadness that is spread over all nature, the deep indestructible melancholy of all life."

Like many other philosophers, deceived by appearances, Schelling fancies savage and dreadful that which is pure, mischevious that which is preservative, and calamitous that which is benign.

The flow of Destruction is as natural and as needful as the flow of water. No human ingenuity can destroy the Immolation of Man, nor prevent the shedding of blood—and why should it?

Majestic Nature continues on her tragic way serenely, caring naught for the wails of the agonized and panic-striken nor the protests of defeat; but smiling sadly, proudly (yet somewhat disdainfully in her passing stride) at the victor's fierce Hurrah. She loves the writhing sword-blades—the rending of tradition, the crunching of bones, and the flap of shredded shot-torn banners, streaming out savagely (in the night, in the day), over the battle-weary, the mangled dying and the swollen dead. Christs may come and Christs may go, but Ceasar lives forever.

Deep, permanent, and abiding is the elemental antagonism between the Sociology of "the Man of Nazareth" and the imprescriptible Laws of the Universe. They are as fire and water to each other—irreconcilable. Indeed our planetary system itself shall melt with fervent heat ere the Gallilean's philosophy can conquer.

No human being can ever hope to attain "the perfectibility that is in Christ." So long as we remain animals, we shall be dominated by animal wants and animal passions and animal rivalries.

Undoubtedly the Messiah ideal is unattainable, hopeless, and especially so upon its reformatory side. However the world loves to be deceived by some ghastly delusion and that is the reason, perhaps, that it has taken to its bosom this rustic fable; this Gospel of Ineffectuality—this Evangel of Darkness—this Dream of an Israelite slave. "When the Assyrians and after them the Medes and Persians," writes Tacitus, "were masters of the Oriental world, the Jews of all nations, then held in subjection, were deemed the most contemptible." Christ was a pariah Jew.

Among the verile conquering tribes, the Ideal Man is ever the all-daring Jove, the splendid Apollo, the self-reliant Achilles, or the Constructive Genius. It is only in centuries of dotage—in ages of cankersome down-going and nervous disease, that the Model Man becomes a Christ. The Model Man of our forefathers was Odin, a War Lord, but our Ideal Man is a weeping, horsewhipped Jew.* A Jew for a God!

The deities of the Greeks and Vikings, Goths and Romans, were all (originally) mighty-men-of-valor, or virile women of surpassing beauty, afterward held up (before their warlike posterity) as splendid examples of natural nobility, conscious power, daring courage, shrewdness, sexual vigor and boundless strength of character. The gods and heros of antiquity spent their vital force in the destruction of monsters, in the seizure of new hunting grounds, in the slaughtering of tyrants and in the breeding of unconquerable sons.

But Christ! the God of Christiandom! the Divine Exemplar! 'that Majestic Figure'! What godlike deed did he ever do? What unconquerable sons did he beget?

If the "first principles of Christianity" should, by an unforeseen miracle, triumph in the elemental conflict that is approaching, assuredly the Anglo-Saxon is played-out, his days numbered, his dominion ended, his sepulchre prepared. Multitudinous multiplication of Unfit Millions (broods of strumous semi-idiots) must then proceed through dreary, barren, brain-paralyzing centuries, winding up perhaps in a blast of pestilential plague—a Black Death.

The "dead and alive" conditions of the "Celestial" Empire will then be applied to this Western World and under the thin disguise of "Advancement," "Progress" and "Civilization," an atmosphere of excruciating torture must be artificially created, hostile to all but degenerative forces, as in China. In the name of "goodness," "righteousness," and "morality," Woe shall be poured out upon our Seed, as it has already been poured out on the rotten Swarms of the Orient.

* "Taunts and blows the portion of the slave." Macauley.

Congenital enfeeblement of body, together with organic degeneracy of mind, must then go on and on, at an ever accelerating ratio, until our posterity may end (as Darwin imagines *we* began) by becoming chattering apes, without sense enough to light a fire, crack a coconut or swing by their tails.

Behold the modern man! this "heir of all the ages—in the foremost ranks of time!" His sight, taste, smell and hearing are all notoriously defective. He can harness thunderbolts, but the unerring instinct of a carrier-pigeon is beyond him. His brain has become an over-heated thinking engine, but he may not read the *Daily Morning Liar*—without spectacles. He "understands" more things (or thinks he does) but if suddenly removed from his artificial environment, he would parish as helplessly as the Babes-in-the-Wood. He can guage sound-waves; photograph broken bones; construct gigantic iron monsters; whisper across miles of copper wire; but, when the pointer-dog sniffs the hidden pheasant from afar off, this erudite Bundle-of-Nerves looks on in blank amazement. The fact is that the civilized man is gradually "losing his senses." If he continues to "progress" at the existing rate, in a comparatively little while, he will have no smell, no sight, no hearing.

"Direr visions worse foreboding,
Glare upon me through the gloom!
Europe's smoke-cloud sinks, corroding
On the land, in noisome fume;
...Showering down like rain of ashes
On the Cities of God's doom.
...Bustling smug, a pigmy pack,
Plucks its prey from ores embraces;
Walks with crooked soul and back:
Glares like dwarfs with greedy eyes,
For the golden glittering lies."*

It is good for a degraded people to be utterly consumed.

 4

In the department of Natural History, it is axiomatic that all kinds of living beings, from protozoa to man, subsist and propagate, through and by the destruction of feebler competitors, belonging to the same species or kindred species.

Thus the big fish eat the little fish—the big trees (by absorbing and monopolizing the nutriment) "eat up" the little trees—the strong animals eat the weak animals and so on—ad infinitum.

* *Henrick Ibsen*—Adapted in the translating.

Man is no exception. Conquering and masterful nations have ever been ravenous devourers of flesh-food; and most of them have also been man-eaters. The slaughter-houses of Christiandom reek with the dying effluvia of millions and millions of butchered brutes; that man—the King of Animals—may day by day eat flesh, drink blood and gnaw bones.

Even cannibalism is not extinct in far lands, nor quite unknown in the centers of our proudest civilizations. With the first great revolutionary cataclysm, its revival upon a gigantic scale is not an improbability.

During the eleventh century, man's flesh was cooked, sold and eaten in England, and Englishmen may again revert to anthropophagy, if ever their imported food supplies should be suddenly and entirely cut off, either by convulsions of nature or acts of war. Shipwrecked crews have repeatedly saved themselves by casting lots and devouring some of their number: and shipwrecked nations (loaded up to the hatches with seething cargos of festering useless nondescripts), may yet be driven to do the same.

Innumerable are the folk-lore legends, relating to ancient and modern man-eaters. Formal human sacrifices upon the Altars of Idols are quite common. In Mexico and Ancient Britain, prelates butchered their victims (generally young virgins) in public, amid the acclaim of musical instruments, the chanting of beautiful liturgies, and the hosanna shouts of the mob.

The modern prelate does not employ the rude smoking gully-knife, but uses other weapons, ten times more keen and more destructive. For every human sacrifice 'offered-up' in olden times, millions are offered now.

🐉 5 🐉

Professor Huxley pictorially describes an African butcher's shop where human steaks, roasts and sirloins, were systematically retailed.

Josephus tells us of mothers who ate their own infants during the last seige of Jerusalem, and in many later seiges human flesh has been consumed.

Oriental traditions record of King Richard Lion Heart, that once upon a time when presiding at a feast of moslem heads, he remarked with grim matter-of-factness "one roast Saracen made good entertainment for nine or ten of my good Christian men." An English Crusading rhymer is even proud of this:

"King Richard shall warrant,
There is no flesh so nourissant,

Unto an English Man;
Partridge, plover, heron, ne swan,
Cow, ne ox, sheep, ne swine,
As the (roast) head of a Sarazan."

Very intelligent New Zealand aboriginals may still be found, who describe with much apparent gusto, how (in comparatively recent dates) they satiated their ravenous hunger, by banqueting all night upon the grilled flesh of foemen they had tomahawked during the day. Neither is it uncommon to hear tattooed old veterans, tell how war-captives were penned up like cattle and fattened upon each other, until required for the tribal oven (formed of red-hot stones, paved into an oval hollow in the ground): how then the fattest were selected one by one, taken out, systematically bled, disembowled and hung up by the heels on neighboring trees; just as sheep, swine and cattle are exposed for sale, in our own abattoirs and meat-markets. The maoris also have a tradition, that if a man kills and eats his enemy, he by doing so, absorbs all the dead man's vitality, strength and courage.

In the nascent Colony of New Zealand, missionaries, soldiers, whalers and pioneers were often cooked and eaten; but by a general consensus of epicurean opinion the 'Pakehas' flesh was voted bad form, principally because it was 'too tough, too salt'.

During the War of Secession, Northern infantrymen accidentally imprisoned in a Virginian mine, devoured each other one at a time; the last man (John Ewing) dying of hunger, and leaving a written record of the facts, sealed up in a flask.

The story of Sawny Bean is well known, also the classical legends of the Cyclops, the Giants, the Phalaris Bull, the Moloch holocausts and Homer's Polyphemus.

Anthropophagy has been practiced in Australia, both by whites and blackfellows. In New Guinea and portions of Africa, man-eating is quite án ordinary custom to this hour. Marcus Clarke describes how Gabbet, an English-born Botany Bay convict, induced his prison comrades to escape with him (into the bush), in order that he might have a holiday and a feast, picking their succulent bones and sucking out the marrow thereof.

All over continental Europe there is a popular superstition that Jew Rabbis steal and murder Christian infants and maidens, in order to use the blood on door-lintels, at Passover and other ceremonials.

A similar charge was brought against the early Christians, and even *proved* in the Imperial Law Courts, if we are to judge by the verdicts.

70

Human fat is regularly retailed in modern drug stores and human heads are even now a marketable commodity in the South Seas. There are also mystic brotherhoods in our midst, whose initiates pledge fidelity, and obligate themselves to life-long secrecy, by drinking blood out of a skull, over emblems of violent death—with daggers pointed at their throats.

The foundation stones of many famous buildings, palaces, castles, temples, and monuments, have been emblematically laid upon the living body of a man—the Kremlin for example.

Is not the Communion Service allegorical anthropophagy? Is it not a pious periodical cannibal feast in more ways than one? Does not the wine symbolize human blood, and the wafers typify human flesh?

Metaphorically considered, every trading Christian State is a meat market, wherein the flesh, bones, and blood not only of men, but of women and little children are bought and sold daily— "offered up" nominally for the "Love of God" really for the Love of Dollars.

Atrocities of the most revolting description are of daily, hourly occurance, not only in Turkey and Siam, but in New York and Chicago; not only in Cuba and Port Arthur, but in London, Madrid, and Paris; not only in Mashonaland, and on the Congo, but in St. Petersburg and Berlin. Men, women, and little children are being everywhere starved slowly to the grave, worked till they fall down, driven insane by legislation, and even tortured to death, inch by inch.

Great financial corporations (backed by the State) directed mostly by Hebrews, literally coin Great Empires into golden dividends: and upon the share lists of mortgage banks and man-devouring institutions generally, may be found the names of bishops, popes, preachers, generals, governors, statesmen—and other human Carnivores by the thousand. He who doubts, should look up the official share registers, and behold the long rows of adorable names belonging to High Priests, Philanthropists and Rulers, appearing thereon.

Cannibalism was practiced in Ancient Greece at the period of highest culture. Herodotus describes Asian feasts where man's flesh was the chief dish: and down to the Thirteenth Century the Thibetans were in the habit of making their parents into broth.

There are confraternaties still in existence, into which no one is ever admitted until he has first killed a man. Among the Dyaks (as among our own ancestors) a youth is never considered a full-grown person capable of founding a home until he has slain at least one enemy in battle. The Thugs of India (a religious sect) brought the science of holy murder, by strategic violence, to such

71

a pitch of perfection that they have never been surpassed—not even by Grant or Moltke.

The Kinderawa of India, make regular practice of eating all their diseased, useless, senile, and decrepit relations: just as packs of wolves fall upon any of their number that is seriously wounded in foray.

In portions of Sumatra, law-breakers are neither imprisoned nor electrocuted, but actually carved up and eaten alive—piece by piece. The Capanagugas of South America make of their own stomachs the sepulchre of their dead relatives. A funeral with them is a banquet—the collation being a corpse. The Terra Del Fuegans throttle and eat all very old women.

The Monbuttas of Central Africa carry on aggressive wars to capture flesh food. They also dry human flitches in the sun and smoke them for export.

During the Tae Ping rebellion, Chinese soldiers (under General Gordon) were in the habit of cutting out and devouring the hearts of their dead enemies (on the battle-field) like the Maoris and Britons.

Mistresses were specially kept by opulent ancient Peruvians, to breed sucklings—for the table. When these women became too old for child-bearing, they were likewise cast into the pot, as useless incumbrances. In 1782 more than forty gypsies were executed in Austria, upon a proved charge of cannibalism. The case of the herdsman Goldsmidt, must not be forgotten; nor the gruesome London legends, regarding sausages being manufactured out of dead cats, dead dogs, dead paupers, and murdered sailors.

The Ancient Scandinavians, Teutons, Celts (vide St. Jerome), Sythians, Mongols, Sarmatians, Cannanites, Goths, and Huns were all anthropophagi.

Indeed the detailed facts of how men have tortured each other for pleasure, revenge or profit, would fill 10,000 volumes. No man in his lifetime could read or comprehend all the horrors that have been perpetrated say in the Tower of London, the Paris Bastile, the Spanish Inquisition, the Rhine Castle Dungeons, by the Bridge of Sighs, the Bosphorous, or in the prison-hells of Chicago, Newgate, Mazas, Siberia, Sing Sing, New Caledonia, Botany Bay or Van Dieman's Land. The cold-blooded cruelty of man to man, surpasses anything that poet-cranks could conceive of as happening in hell.

Cannibalism undoubtedly originated amid over-crowded populations in some pre-historic age. Among moderns (civilized and savage) it merely exists as a survival choice of social conditions which have long since passed away. At some former era of the world's profoundly mysterious history, men-animals increased in swarming myriads as they are doing now; until at last on the surface of the soil there was scarcely standing room for all. Then the air became laden with the reeking effluvia of their strumous bodies, breeding decimating pestilences, cholera, small-pox, leprosy, poisoning the wells and rivers, and transforming Babylons into charnel houses and tombs. The rearing of tame cattle for food in such an environment probably became too expensive and cumbersome. Perhaps even the cattle would also be swept away by some blight or rinderpest. Under such horrible circumstances, survivors might from necessity resort to anthropophagy. Gradually, the new habit would grow upon them and become a settled custom.

The segmental fragments of pre-historic civilizations are—the Cannibal Savages of to-day—the savages that we are displacing, pushing aside in order that we may enslave them and repeat over again the same weary old round of growth, power and decay.

Shiploads of dead soldiers, dug out of old battle-fields, possess a regular commercial value. They are imported into England, to be chemically treated and manufactured into fertilizers for enriching exhausted wheat fields. Human hair commands a steady sale, and "cadavers" may be bought for dissection, in any great city for a dollar, C.O.D.

The tanning of human skins for glove-making and book-binding (Meudon!) is an old-established industry.

The transfusion of blood from animals into human veins, from healthy humans into unhealthy ones (for a price), is regularly practiced by medical men. The grafting of flesh, bone, and skin, has also been successfully performed.

American sheriffs and detectives hunt down tramps and criminals with specially trained bloodhounds, just as Russians hunt wolves, and sheepfarmers hunt coyotes and dingos. It is nowise unusual for Negroes to be first captured, then chained to a stake, flayed alive, soaked in kerosene, and burnt to death amid exultant shrieks of corybantic delight.

Roman Senators fattened their lampreys and eels upon the drowned bodies of old worn out slaves; and patrician maids and matrons (with uplifted thumb), sent many a gladiator to kingdom come. For innate cruelty of deed, no animal can surpass woman.

In Mahomedan Europe, boys are unsexed by the lancet, that they may thereafter be more safely employed as harem-attendants, and in Christian Europe "eunuchs are made and trained and priced, to sing the praise of risen Christ."

Young girls are nightly bought and sold for currency, like horses and hogs, at the street corners: and upon the profits of licensed polyandry "pillars of the church" become millionaires. Even the salaries of fuminating evangelists are paid out of Rahab's rent.

Baths of human blood are not unknown to students of history: and Jack the Ripper, with his letters written in harlots' blood, enclosing pieces of fried woman's liver to the London Chief of Police, is certainly a fabulous ancient legend.

Is this the record of a breed of "dearly beloved bretheren"? What hollow mockery these holy phrases are, to be sure?—The Brotherhood of man! Ha! Ha! The Brotherhood of Devils rather!

Allegorically speaking the clothes we wear—the houses we live in—the food we eat—the books we read, have been carved (by force) out of other men's bones and flesh. Literally they are the hides, sinews, flesh, pulp, and outer woolen covering of captive animals, transmuted by human slavery into garments, lumber, implements, thoughts, shoes, and daily dinners. Indeed man's tushes are against all other animate beings whatsoever; and in turn, their fangs are against him. So it goes on, and on, and on, as merrily as marriage bells. Viae Victus! And behold, it is good! This world is no Nirvana, where peaceful pleasure flows. It is a gruesome butcher-shop, where slain men hang in rows.

🐉 6 🐉

From the scientific point of view, it is but a single step from the eating of captive cattle, horses, sheep, hares, rabbits, deer, hogs, etc., to the eating of captive men.

It may grate upon the unstrung nerves to be harshly told these gruesome facts in straight language. However, calm sensible readers must unreservedly admit that Man is not a pretty, harmless little cherub; not even a "lamb," but the fiercest, most ferocious, most cunning, and most bloodthirsty of all the vertebrates. He is the fighting, roving, pillaging, lusting, cannibalistic animal, par excellence—the King of the Great Carnivores. When *he* takes his walks abroad, the "wild beasts" of the field and the birds of the air, even the most courageous of them, are stricken dumb. Shuddering they fly from his shadow (or his odor down the wind) hiding in trembling and quaking with terror.

It is man's destructive energy—not his altruism, that makes him absolute monarch of all he surveys; and yet, how feeble he is if compared to the powers of Nature that gave him being? No other beast will stand and face him, except it cannot run away—not even a snake, a tiger, or a wolf.

Structurally, men are fashioned for purposes of inflicting and suffering pain. Every human anatomy is an elaborate nerve and bone infernal machine—a kind of breathing, perambulating Juggernaut—a superb engine of lethal immolation that automatically stokes its furnace fires with its victims.

Men rush upon each other (or upon their prey) with hoarse war-shouts and bloodshot eyes, as prowling beasts of the deserts and jungles do. Man banquets upon his quarry with greediness, snarling, and growling with ferocious triumphant delight, just like unto wolves: but HE loves to act the hypocrite—turn up the whites of his protesting eyes to 'heaven'—weep crocodile tears over his mangled, bleeding and palpitating carrion. How exultantly he lilts his Te Deum, his Kyrie Eleison, his Et in terra pax, his Glorias, and his Alleluias; while with blood-clotted jaw and distended paunch he licks his gaping wounds?

As the painted Redskin chants his vengeful ghost-song, so the furious Paleface whoops his double-leaded editorial. As the hungry lion roars at midnight on African karoo, or in Himalayan jungle, so the piratical Anglo-Teuton roars his 'Battle Hymn of the Republic' his 'Britania Rules the Waves,' or his 'Watch by the Rhine.' Exactly as the Moslem fanatic yells "Allah Akbar," while slicing up hated "Christian dogs," so the vicious Englishman thunders forth his "Hip, Hip Hurrah!" while driving an elegant bayonet-dagger into the liver of "wicked heathens"; whose property he thereafter annexes—as a matter of course, for "business is business, don't you know."

Man's anatomy, external and internal; his eyes, his teeth, his muscles, his blood, his viscera, his brain, his vertebrae; all speak of fighting, passion, aggressiveness, violence, and prideful egoism.

Even the component elements of a human body are themselves in a constant state of internecine warfare. Our bony framework and pulsating tissues, are vast campaign grounds; whereon microscopical animal-culae in countless myriads, fight out their ephemeral lives, as we ourselves do—with tooth and claw. When one swarm of microbes, germs, or spores, conquer (in the struggle for sustenance) disease, or death supervenes to us, as the case may be. When rival hosts vanquish, then our flesh, nerves, bones, and blood become *their* happy hunting grounds, and our health returns—at least until the bacilli-batallions have finally eaten us out: or they have been, themselves, conquered and exterminated by fiercer swarms.

It is not improbable that this earth itself is a living breathing organism and that the Tribes of Man are microbes and bloodsucking vermin (on its outer cuticle) imagining themselves "the whole thing." Just as itch-creating parasites burrow into our own hide, so (in our turn) we may be unpleasant parasites, burrowing in the hide of some nobler and grander Being.

75

🐉 7 🐉

From youth to hoary age, man takes an instinctive delight in all that pertains to warfare and the chase.

As a boy he twangs his arrows at the sparrows, trains and loads his toy-cannon, marshals his tin soldiers, brandishes his wooden sword, fights his mimic battles, builds his snow fortifications on the play ground; and the proudest day of his life is that on which he becomes the proprietor of "a real gun."

As a full grown citizen he practices homicide with repeating rifle, at moving targets—slaughters tame pigeons with choke-bore breechloaders—hunts foxes, wolves, bears, pumas, over mountain and mere—wades up to his neck in swamps to kill teal, and travels to far lands in search of Big Game and nigger shooting.

The Indian fighters of North America take supreme joy in slaying red devils; and to "pot a blackfellow" in Queensland is boasted of round campfires under gum trees, as—"great fun."

The Cape of Good Hope, Australia, New Zealand, North and South America, have been made into veritable human shambles and gory hunting grounds, within the memory of middle-aged men. Indeed the delight which men take in slaying wild animals, is tameness itself, compared with the exultation they display in hunting, trailing and slaughtering each other.

Man-hunts were organized systematically in Lacadamon, when the helots became too numerous and too restive. It is not improbable that as our own surplus "submerged tenths" increase in numbers, they may be thinned out by similar battues.

At every meal we rend flesh, scrape bones, suck marrow, and daintily lap blood; just as our hairy troglodyte progenitors did. The food supply of all Christian nations is composed of the body and blood—the hides and marrow of *both* human herds and vast swarms of inferior brutes, living, dying, dead. The lives of countless hordes of hirelings, are daily being transmuted into juicy steaks and sirloins; that those who have money may buy and eat thereof. Not only do we ferociously compete for our prey, i.e., for subsistence; but we literally eat each other with voracity, relish, and mutual toleration. Thus properly understood, Darwinism is no very comforting doctrine for fat men.

Public buildings and frowning fortresses; capitols and prisons; "temples of freedom" and cross-crowned cathedrals, have (every one of them) been constructed upon exactly the same general principles whereby the Pyramids of On and the Palaces of Ninevah were built—every riveted girder, every iron transom, every block of

76

concrete, every solid, squared, and polished stone, has been bedded literally in a dying groan; by the hands of dehumanized and conquered decadents, insensate—"of reason void, of reverence full."

There is nothing immoral, nothing abnormal, in these grim facts. All is in strict harmony with that cosmic enactment—the Survival of the Strongest.

In the proud language of Germany's chansonist:

"The living current through the air is heaving,
Breathing blessings, see them bending;
Balanced worlds from change defending,
While everywhere diffused is harmony unending."

Instinctively we understand that the struggle for existence is absolutely needful. We feel that Nature makes no mistakes, and therefore we accept her dicta *because we must:* not because it has been eloquently formulated, by sublimated visionaries; or re-echoed, again and again, by thousands of human microphones.

❈ 8 ❈

When not thwarted by artificial contrivances, whatever argument Nature promulgates is—*right*. The further man gets away from Nature, the further he departs from right. To be right is to be natural, and to be natural is to be right. The sun shines, therefore it is right that it should shine—the rain falls, therefore it is right that it should fall—the tides ebb and flow, therefore it is right that they should ebb and flow.

Darwin's law exists—may be seen in operation—is practicable—of daily demonstration—therefore it also is right. It is not a dream like "Religion," it is not an invention like "Morals," it is not an assumption like "God." It is a cosmic Fact, like the sunshine, the rain, and the tides! Nature does not set up Idols, does not found Superstitions, does not invent Decalogues. These toys and fetters have been constructed by man, for his own infinite—damnation.

Neither morals, laws, nor creeds are First Principles, but they may (probably) have their uses; just as guillotines, and gardeners' hoes have *their* uses. They may be convenient engines for the deletion of Lower Organisms, for extripating individuals of infantile intellect. Indeed the secret object of all superstitions possibly is, to provide an ultra-rational sanction for fraudulent standards of Right and Wrong.

To base a Lie upon a Myth, is certainly much safer than to base it on a Reality, for you cannot run a tape-measure over a Myth.

Christliness, as social quietism, has never yet been accepted by men of super-eminent strength, courage, and wisdom. Such men have everywhere regarded the Christ Ideal as a model for slavish souls *only*—to be humored for strategic purposes but never practiced by masters, conquerors, kings. "Don't do as I *do*, but do as I *say*" has ever been the dicta of High Priests and Rulers—to docile multitudes.

The evolution of sovereignty satisfactorily exhibits this ethical dictatorship, as an historical commonplace. Moral codes (always and everywhere *imposed* upon the common people by "immoral" combinations of cumulative craft) are never obeyed by Ruling Castes.

✵ 9 ✵

If the Masters of Christiandom are to be judged by Moral Codes, by the Common Law, or by Gospel Injunctions, there is not one 'moral' individual among them. Measured by Religio-Ethical dogmas, they are one and all, an amalgamated Mafia of Blackmailers, confidence-men, thieves, murderers, and infidels. *As far as the codes are concerned,* honesty must undoubtedly be searched for among the dregs of society, rather than among the elite. But it is essentially unjust to measure the Conquerers of Mankind by fallacious Christly standards. Christ, together with his moral measuring rod, is their subordinate agent—an effective instrument of State.

Indeed, "Moral Principles" are one of the tricks in the game of "dog eat dog" all are playing. They are effectively narcotized out of the deal, who fancy themselves "Safe in the arms of Jesus."

Never yet has there been a Christian king, a Christian president, a Christian congress, nor a Christian synod. Of course many prominent celebreties have professed Christianism—for example: Judas Iscariot, St. Peter, Torquemada, Cromwell, Abraham Lincoln, Napoleon, Gladstone, and Jabez Spencer Balfour; but only minds paralytic judge of men by professions. Christian and Ruler are direct contradictions.

The ridiculous ineffectuality of all Gospel Theories, shows that they were only invented as campaign lies.

Christ explicitly condemns the use of force, and yet all existent nations (without exception) were founded by unlimited throat-cutting and piracy. The rulers of the world, the directors of concentrated Power, are not now, and never have been, sad-eyed Saviours—mournful, immaculate tramp-gods—but masters of majestic violence. To use the language of Isaiah, not only Zion, but every nation on earth "has been built with blood." Nations cannot be built otherwise.

The Romans first appear in history as a gang of banditti—the English as a nest of pirates—the Germans as a horde of roving freebooters—the Russians as a band of mounted horse-thieves—the Americans as pious anarchists and nigger stealers—the Australians as exiled cut-purses—the Turks as Bedouin brigands.

Everywhere the symbol of kingship, tribal totems, and insignia of state, speak of Violence, Defiance and War.

The fasces carried before a Roman Praetor, consisted of an axe for chopping necks, and a bundle of rods for whipping backs. The Mace of the English parliamentary organization, of which the American system is an imitative offshoot ("that bauble of Cromwell") also all Royal Sceptres are but carved and gilded clubs. Originally both Mace and Sceptre were in daily use for breaking recalcitrant skulls. They are still emblematic of Legislative Authority—and offensive Violence—as much so indeed, as the knotted bludgeon, the barbed lance, or the greenstone skull-splitter of an orthodox cannibal chief.

National crests are selected, not as a rule from doves, lambs, goats, magpies, and hares; but from lions, tigers, she-wolves, serpents, dragons, bears, eagles, and the Fighting Man.

In the centers of "our highest civilization," force is recognized as the underlying principle of Authority. Between nation and nation it is in constant requisition, as the basis of all diplomacy, and between contending factions (within the nation) it is often effectively applied. The policeman's loaded truncheon, the huzzar's slicing sabre, and the artillery company's field piece, are still the ultimo ratio of Order, Liberty, Peace. The maxim-gun is a development, and a decided improvement upon the old time bludgeon; especially when dealing with rabid revolutionary masses. One of those beautiful engines and half a dozen trained men, if supplied with plenty of ammunition, could wipe out in half a day, the largest mob of would-be insurgents that London, Paris or Chicago ever saw. "We have found in most cases that one regiment of regular infantry, is quite capable of managing the biggest and wildest mob," write millionaire editor Kohlsaat. *Chicago Times-Herald* (13-11-96).

When citizens disobey legal "regulations" they are generally interviewed at first, by a blue-coated 'guardian of the Peace," with an official warrant and a varnished club, who tamely leads them away to a State dungeon, or indicts them before a State Inquisitor. Behind the armed police and the suave Judge, stand in threatening array, the whole military and naval forces of Government and Law.

Law Courts and Thrones are (de facto) built upon bayonets. Likewise all Statutes, Constitutions, and Moral Codes are written by the Sword. Material Strength is now, and ever has been, and ever must be, the true basis upon which all political institutions rest. No other foundation is feasible.

What the sword has established the sword must defend. Symbolic thereof, every emperor and president, every sultan, king, shah, or savage chief, is proclaimed before drilled legions and raucous multitudes; amid the fan-fare of battle trumpets—the unsheathing of battle-sword—and the thundering roar of battle-cannon. Two examples, from two continents—from two different systems of Government—may be quoted as sufficient proof of this:

Sir Edwin Arnold describes the recent Coronation of the Emperor of Russia, an hereditary absolute monarch: "Behind and between the royal chairs, stood the new Commander of the silver-eagle regiment, his saber bared and gleaming." When cannon volleys, booming across two continents, from Riga to Vladivostock, announced the final crowning of their Suzerain, 2,000,000 Sclavonian warriors bared their heads in acknowledgement, clanged their weapons in token pride, and swore eternal allegiance.

"Governor John R. Tanner (of Illinois), mounted on a black horse, and wearing a broad-brimmed felt hat, with gold braid and tassel (also calvary saber), will ride down Pennsylvania Avenue (Washington) at the head of the First Regiment...National Guards, in the President's inaugural...crack Illinois soldiery marching...next the President's Personal Escort...Troop A. 8th Infantry...Along with the regiment will go the gun corps and the gatling guns that did service...during the Debs insurrection." The President of these United States, an elective Monarch, is Commander-in-Chief of the federal armed forces, and possesses more administrative authority than any Asiatic despot.

Every military and naval officer in England receives his commission direct from the Queen, and until recently it was customary at Coronation ceremonials for an hereditary Champion (armed cap-a-pie) to ride out into the courtyard and there, before assembled commoners, knights, nobles, generals, officially challenge to personal encounter, anyone who dared to even question the royal titles.

European land-title deeds may be (in every instance) traced back to military and kingly power. In all the English colonies, waste lands are occupied and cleared, under "Crown grants." The same principle prevails in this Republic and among all savage tribes.

🦅10🦅

By force all things that exist are evolved, maintained and perpetuated. Force aggregates and separates the atoms that go to make up this cosmic universe of mind and matter. It integrates them into forms, organic and inorganic. It disintegrates them again and again. It builds up and pulls down, without the slightest respect to man's wishes or desires. It theorizes, creates, constructs, annihilates, attacks, and repels. It is literally in all, through all, and *over* all.

Even the undulatory migration of races, that now proceeds (over sea and continent), in great animalistic waves, as it did in the days of Akbar and Tamerlane, is also the vibrations of force, acting through human media. It is the incarnate pulsations of Power.

Antiquarian delvings in America, Europe, Africa, Asia and the Islands of the Sea, corroborate the written annals, folk-lore, and legends of tribes and nations. The past of this pendant ball, is one long awe-inspiring chronicle of cannibalisms, invasions, ravishments, cataclysms, "battle, murder and sullen death."

The surface of the soil is a lethal chamber—the bottom of the sea a charnel house. Both are littered from pole to pole with the ruins of forgotten "civilizations" that men and nature have delighted to destroy. Everywhere and always the debilitated have perished, everywhere and *always* the mightiest have won. As it was in the beginning, is now, and ever shall be, Power, Slavery, Pain, Joyounce, side by side.

Races of Helots are never wanting! See to it O Men, that you breed fighters! See to it that you train them too! "The harper is not made otherwise than by harping" nor the warrior otherwise than by war. Let muscle force be pitted against muscle force, brain power against brain power and let winners wear the laurel and losers wear the rasping sackcloth. Let there be no compromise— no half-hearted philandering—no backing down but as Darwin commands, let the strongest live and the vilest die.

Black, furious and tragic are the bloody annals of man's evolution, and there is no rational evidence upon which to conclude that it shall ever be otherwise—or that it would be wise for us to attempt the making of it otherwise.

Why then be discontented with that which we cannot alter, even if we dared? Better after all, fifty years of Europe than a cycle of Cathay. Let it be as it has ever been—as the grim old Norseland skald chanted it, when our Race began to emerge into the dim distant twilight of the gods.

81

"An age of axes—an age of swords;
An age of tempests—an age of wolves."

Be it among animalculae, moth or mollusc, birds of the air, beasts of the field, fish of the sea, planets, suns, stars or solar systems; *Force* reigns unchangeable, unchallengeable, inexorable.

When the kindly Roman emperor imagined that peace had settled down permanently upon the ancient world, even then, the (dissimulating) assassin's dagger was sharpening for his throat: and now, while Lower Organisms dream of a "world of lovers"—of arbitration instead of hostility—of conciliation between rival carnivores; the mechanism of deletion is silently under construction: that (when completed) will sweep them off the face of the earth.

The Strongest organisms are always the determinants. They hold in their hands (absolutely) the destinies of weaker organisms. Further, in all the interwoven differentiations of matter and mind, equality, mercy, pity are wholly at discount—except alone in family relationship. (A man's family is his property—it is part of himself. Therefore his *natural* business is to defend it, as he would his own life. Women and children *belong* to man, who must hunt for them as well as for himself. He is their lord and master, in theory and in fact.)

Under natural conditions, there is no haven for the wretched, no hope for the weaklings, no resting place for the weary, no quarter for the beaten. Nature loathes Infirm Ones. Every organism, every human being, must conquer or serve. This is an Ultimatum.

Life is a race for Power into the very jaws of death and "hell take the hindmost."

Hell take the hindmost! No!—that isn't so! Christ take the hindmost! Exactly! that is correct! In real life *he* is the true Prince of Evil. Soothingly he saith: "Come unto me all ye that are weary or heavy laden," and, those who obey are sure of—hell. Nay, they are already in it! "The smoke of their torment ascendeth up for ever and ever."

In ancient ages the Incapables were permitted to perish without comment: but with us it is different.

Almsgiving, first by the monastery, now by the State, has preserved them and their leprous seed, until modern nations are actually swarming with men and women (rich and poor) totally useless and totally vile. Selective influences that operate under natural conditions, have been kept in abeyance by religions and moralisms: until the whole human race is saturated with inherited mental disease and rottenness-of-the-bones. Our Christian civilization is a forcing-chamber for weakly animalculae. Natural conditions are a lethal chamber for them. The proper home for incurables is—the grave.

Competition must be to the death. If retarded in any way it fails of beneficial results. The chief intent of false religions and false moralisms is to arrest competition half-way to safeguard degenerates in possessing that which they could neither seize nor defend if competition were unlimited. Humanitarian institutionalisms have been invented to handicap and eliminate the elite of mankind—vainly, however.

With the *normal* man, it is a pleasure to struggle, a pastime to fight, and nothing is sweeter to him than to confiscate his confiscator and surpass his surpasser—to, as it were, smite his enemy hip and thigh and spoil him of that which he spoiled from others. The normal man prefers to eat others than to be eaten.

With the *abnormal* man, it is otherwise. He is of the mob—and sheepishly obeys public opinion—he is one of a flock. That word flock!—Does it not postulate the existence of shepherds to "round-up" and drove—of specialists to castrate—of shearers to shear—of cattle dealers to purchase—of butchers to kill—of tanneries—wire fences—corrals—abattoirs; and finally of "roast lamb and mint sauce," with fat Carnivores sitting round, lapping blood and purring gently?

11

Herbert Spencer (referring to the origin of manners, customs, and political institutions) says: "The will of the victorious chief, of the strongest, was the rule of all conduct. When he passed judgment on private quarrels, his decisions were the origin of law. The mingled respect and terror inspired by his person and his peerless qualities, then deemed super-natural by the rude minds that had scarcely an idea of the powers and limits of human nature, were the origins of religions, and *his* opinions were the first dogmas. The signs of obedience by which the vanquished, whom he spared, repaid his mercy, were the first examples of those marks of respect that are now called good manners and forms of courtesy."

How human history duplicates itself over and over again? How it revolves in a never ending panorama?

Wherever human herd congregate, the "Victorious Chief" still governs, though not without envy and impotent opposition. Everywhere he is Master in one guise or another: but it behooves him to beware that his power is not undermined by the teredo of sanctified utopianism—founded on the multitudinous votes of the vile, the vulgar, and the vitiated. Blighting indeed is the tyranny of Collective Humanity.

"The great political superstition of the present," also writes Spencer, is "the divine right of parliaments and the implied divine right of majorities."

The supremacy of Living Manhood over devout dreaming, over literature, dogma, law and tradition, must be boldly asserted and aggressively maintained, as it was in the days of yore. Woe unto you Strong Ones if ever you get beneath the hoofs of the trampling, bellowing, maddened mob. Ha!—'You must meet the guile and death-snare with battle and with wrack'.

"Woe to the vanquished, was stern Brenno's word, when sank proud Rome beneath the Gallic sword. Woe to the vanquished, when his massive blade bore down the scales against her ransom weighed: and on the field of foughten battle still, woe knows no limits—save the victor's will."

"The Survival of the Fittest" is the scientists' translation of the heroic age's "Viae Victus." Grim and harsh it may appear to nervous souls, but it is *true to nature.* Neither legislative enactments nor pious incantations can deflect or nullify it. It may be thwarted and turned aside for a time, but only for a time; just as a river may be banked back by the building of a breastwork. The waters cease to flow onward until the dam is brim-full, and then, over the top the flood leaps, with resounding crash and uproar, finally sweeping away the obstruction itself.

Decalogues and "be it enacteds" are mud ramparts the decadent ages vainly erect against the irresistible flow of natural events. Sooner or later these feeble barriers go down, or are surmounted, just as the river surmounts the dam. Cardinal Newman tersly describes the Church of England as a "serviceable breakwater" and he speaks with astuteness. All sacredotalisms are "serviceable breakwaters." They may last for one century or twenty, but they down-tumble in the end. Artificial obstructions cannot last for if they did, the cankerous ancient civilizations would never have been overwhelmed; for they also had their serviceable breakwaters, that is to say, gods and temples, mob-politics, mob-morals, mob-philosophies.

Legal and ethical barricades may not be depended upon to protect dwindlings from the judgments they bring upon themselves, and which they richly deserve.

Every People that have been blotted-out, were rightfully blotted-out. What a frightful maggot-heap this earth would now be, if the "civilized" populations of the past had not perished? If nature had permitted them to live and multiply and propagate their "progress," that is to say, their iniquity, what a noisome sink it would be? What must Futurity be like, if wars and plagues do not come, burning up contemporary infernalisms and purifying the air?

Thus, the utter extermination of enfeebled breeds is in accordance with the Highest Wisdom: and whether we personally approve thereof or not, it must persist. There is nothing unjust, nothing ultra-natural, nothing diabolic about the elimination of the vile—to make room for the "sound in mind and limb."

Clearly, therefore, in every department of life, the lesser force must be overthrown by the greater, which (being interpreted) meaneth: *Might is Right*, absolutely, unreservedly. From the records of history, the facts of life, and the discoveries of science, this startling deduction may be thoroughly proved. "The law of life," as Benjamin Kidd writes, "has been always the same from the beginning, ceaseless and inevitable struggle, ceaseless and inevitable selection and rejection." That 'Might is Master' should require demonstrating is in itself a proof of the mental and moral perversity that pervades the world. Perhaps, however, the 'age we live in,' may not be an 'age of enlightenment and progress,' but an age of darkness, arrested development, and psychic paralysis. Mayhap the theologies and intellectualisms of our time may be but a magical hoodwink. We might (for example) be enchanted on the down-grade track, that leads to eternal extinction, while insanely imagining "progress and enlightenment." Also the imagining process may be part of the complicated mechanism that facilitates the descent—the descent into Sheol. Official statistics show that racial deterioration (begun centuries ago as a sequence of ultra-naturalism) is now preceding at a tremendous rate.

Dr. Haycraft, F.R.S.E., in his book *Darwinism and Race Progress* asserts "there are strong grounds for believing that during the last 30 years, the race has decidedly degenerated." The decadence of character is obvious to the most obtuse understanding, especially in this land of Liberty and Light, where you can buy statesmen with a snuff-box—editors with a dollar and—women with a gew-gaw.

Udoubtedly degenerative forces prevail in our social life, and yet it is impressed upon us from our youth up, that: "A Great Light hath come down upon the earth and all the ends of the world hath seen the Salvation of our God." Salvation indeed! What lunacy?

"So the multitude goes, like the flower and the weed
That wither away to let others succeed—
So the multitude comes, even that we behold;
To repeat every tale that has often been told."

To act as the hunted ostrich on an African karoo—to hide our heads from a cosmic vengeance in hot pursuit, is as futile and ridiculous as it is base. No empiric reorganization of the social system—no rock of ages—no legislative memorialism—no fungus virtues—no scheme of fool redemption—no patent economic plan—no Israelitish codes of "Thou Shalts" and 'Thou Shalt Nots," can deliver whimpering defectives from the wrath that is their just reward. Sooner or later *their* "Day of Judgment" cometh, bringing in its train desolation, reparation and rolling doom.

Even as I write—with wrecked civilization laying around men, cold and chill—outraged Nature is preparing her whirlblasts of wholesale avengement. Europe is a vast powder magazine, with a strident maniac in the middle waving a burning torch; and from Asia is wafted the odorous stench of plague-smitten millions.

Any day, any hour, "Civilization" may be startled from its hypnotic trance, to gaze upon the mightiest drama that has ever been unrolled when 'the tempest flings out its red banner of lightning,' and great nations groan, and reel, and surge, and rock; beneath the thunderous tread of trampling legions, drilling for the savage shock. Military arsenals are preparing in every city, and floating defiantly on Seven Seas are the steel-clad fortresses of rival MIGHTS.

Foolish and blind (or mad) are they who think the struggle for existence ended. It is only begun. This Planet is in its infancy, not in its decrepitude. The 'end of all things' is afar off. The kingdom of heaven is *not* at hand. Incessant is the rivalry for supremacy among men, and manifold are its metamorphoses. Not for a single hour, for a single second, is there an armistice. Night and day the combat rages, and with renewed virulence on Sundays. When we fall asleep and when we wake up, the clashing of the weapons and the crunching of the bones, is sounding on our ears. Everywhere "the sword is uplifted on man." Everywhere Cain's bludgeon is cracking skulls, and with bloodhounds Americans hunt each other. The hands of "Congregations of the Faithful" are red with the blood of the innocent; yet how they boast of being washed clean in the blood of their Brother—the Lamb.

Eternal battle is the main condition upon which man holds his life tenure. When the brand is shattered in his hand, that is death or—slavery. When his enemies are beneath his heel, that is life, honor, success. Indeed the struggle between men is more pitiless, and more unmerciful, than among brutes.

The brute beasts do not enslave, but permit the unfit to die off. Man enslaves his "brother man" on business principles, and makes fuel of the widow and the fatherless. The "failures in life" may be counted by millions and everyone knows their horrible fate—their living death. Behold them being whirled into the blazing maw of the great iron furnaces.

Overt action is not always needful for the drastic removal of lower organisms. Very often, if left alone, degenerates cremate themselves. If given control of governmental mechanisms, they immediately commence to grind one another into mincemeat (that is to say, into dividends), crying Holy! Holy! Holy! Mentally, physically, morally, they are past redemption. Doomed souls are they—miserable sinners!

Seventy-five percent of the inmates of state orphan asylums (for example) are the children of parents that perish from chronic alcoholism. Poverty, helotism, are results of chronic ballot-boxing. Alcoholism and politics are convenient Destructives— Crematories; whereby weak-minded "flocks" may eliminate themselves with beneficial results—

Nature having already condemned them, they provide each other with palatable poisons—for slow but sure suicide. They build gehenna-fires and cast themselves headlong into blazes.

Sociology is a biological problem and Nations are herds of cattle. How much demagogic he-hawing would die down into solemn self-questioning if this Grim Omnific Fact was clearly realized?

BE AS A LION IN THE PATH!

Hate for hate and ruth for ruth,
Eye for eye and tooth for tooth.
Scorn for scorn and smile for smile,
Love for love and guile for guile.
War for war and woe for woe,
Blood for blood and blow for blow.

Thou hast listened full oft, to the diabolic philosophy of the 'Divine Creepling!': 'Love your enemies and bless them that hate you and despitefully use you.'

But I say unto you: Love thy kindred, love thy friends, love thyself, and hate thine enemies with a whole heart.

Be you a foe to your friend's foe—a friend to your friend's friend, and above all things permit no wrong, done unto thee or thine, to pass unchallenged, unredressed, unavenged.

Let thy motto be: "Tread not on me."

For he that tamely submits, to insult and injury is worse than a dog: he is a dastard, a born slave, a Christling.

I'm the friend of all brave men,
The foe of all cowards;
I call up high daring,
I cast down despair.

An Evil Spirit hath innoculated our race with the hideous gospel of submissiveness, of degeneracy:

'Resist all evil' it whines and 'If a man smite thee on one cheek, turn to him the other also.'

But I say unto you: 'If a man smite you on one cheek, smash *him* on 'the other.'

Resist every Evil! Be as a lion in the path! Be 'dangerous' even in defeat!

Courage, I say! Courage! and evermore Courage!

Even the stars in their courses are fight for the bold.

5

THE CHIEF END OF MANHOOD

"You must tread on the necks of your enemies if you would win renown. It is success that makes the great man " was Napoleon's dicta. The whole duty of man in this world is to *succeed*—to help himself, defeat his foes, outstrip his rivals. He who conquers not, is conquered. He who is unable to trample rough-shod over others, will assuredly be trampled over by them. In the strength of his arm man eats his bread. In the sweat of his brow (and brain), the slave earns bread—for a master.

All emotional rhetoric about "love one another," "learn to labor and to wait," etc., has a tendency to paralyze effort—to make victims rather than victors of assentients. Every man's hand *is* against every other man; *except* where *living* individuals have formed temporary co-partnerships. When one partner breaks the mutual agreement, then the Combine is necessarily dissolved, and all become enemies—as before. Fraternity between carnivores is as transient as the smoke of the morning. It is a pro-tem expedient.

Two hungry lions may engage to hunt together, but should one attempt to seize more than his fair proportion of the prey, then it is—woe to the vanquished.

Self preservation first, foremost, above all things, and *at whatever cost*, is the law of the jungle. So must it be among human carnivores. So it is, for society is a jungle. Therefore O reader! Go forth and win! Possess all you can of earth's good things. Man *does* live by bread alone. Be strong and fear not, for all obstruction melts away before real strength of deed and strength of character. Nothing succeeds like success. Do not quibble over the order of your succeeding but—succeed. Thou shalt give thy heart to no god, for that is idiocy; neither shalt thou love thy neighbors as thyself, for that is madness. Let "Nil Desperandum" be your motto even to the death. If you fail you are righteously detestable; but if you triumph, thrice blessed art thou. (The great vice of our age is cowardice.) Glory and honor be unto him that wins, but anathema maranatha be upon the head of him that fails. Failure is not only a disgrace, but practical proof of organic incompetence.

Power and proprietorship cover a multitude of sins—of *alleged* sins: but men and women (especially women), have an overflowing fund of sympathy and forgiveness—for the "Bold Bad Man" if he is victorious. How women admire men of leonine resolution and Eagle Principles. How they detest cowardice, "goodness," feebleness, effeminacy, failure. There is no character in history so universally applauded as the bold "bad" rebel and the mighty conquerer.

Therefore get you gold and land and power somehow. If foiled and baffled one way, try another. Where there's a will there are a thousand ways. If the worn and beaten tracks are intentionally blockaded against you, do not hesitate to cut-out a new highway through the jungle—for yourself. Never mind the pulpiteers and editors. They are hired to blind and blockade you. Above all things do not follow the multitude, for it tramples downward, ever downward along Via Del Mortes to abysses of poverty, chains, and shame. Retreat not, turn not aside to the right hand nor to the left, but zig-zag on. Ask no quarter, no sympathy. "Die the death" rather than surrender and perishing—strike at your conqueror. "Withhold not good from him to whom it is due, when it is in the power of thine hand to do it." But withal be honorable and upright, never forgetting that bravery (which includeth all other virtues) is the highest wisdom—and material success the chief end of man. 'Upward thou must rise, or falter—bend the neck or stand triumphant—be the anvil or the hammer.'

Battle and conquer *here and now*, for behold!—to-morrow you die! you die!—and that *is* the end of you. Let Napoleon's ideal be thine. Napoleon was Darwin on horseback. When addressing the ragged and famishing army of Italy, these were his words: "*Soldiers*! abundance courts you in the fertile plains below (the plains of Italy) ... are you deficient in constancy and courage?" Events proved that they were not deficient in constancy and courage.

Consequently the spoils of Italy and the stored-up treasures of the great Venetian Bank were equalized among them. Everywhere similar conditions have prevailed absolutely, and always will prevail. There is land for the taking, and gold for the raking, and fame and power, and song, for the brave, the bold and the strong— *and for none other*. Therefore, be thou a Napoleon—don't be a Christ.

90

Get you Property by whatever method comes easiest to you. Reverting to terms economic 'buy power in the cheapest market and sell it in the dearest.' Gratify your life-hopes as the lions and eagles do, i.e., along the lines of least resistance—even as do growing plants in a dark cellar. Do they not endeavor to reach sunshine by the most direct route?

Scorn all insolent dictation as to right and wrong. Decide right and wrong for yourself. Get property, honestly if you can, but remember "business is business." ("Mr. Cecil Rhodes under heavy fire for fifteen minutes, captured one herd of cattle himself."*) Life is life and defeat is hell. Obey thine Inner Voice! It can never err. It is thy very soul. Be a Darwin in active operation. Do noble deeds, don't dream about them all thy life long.

'Moral principles' you say! What are moralisms that they should paralyze your arm and brain? Are they not artificial human enactments, apparently sanctified, but not necessarily natural, honest, just or true? Moral codes are the Black Terror of all dastards.

The ethical principles of Christiandom, judging by daily developments, are the principles of a mocking, sneaking hypocritic devil—if there is a devil.

Readers must distinctly understand theat *sexual morality* is nowise condemned in these pages. In all sexual relations (as in everything else) "morality" is what Strength decrees. Women are frail beings at the best of times and in their secret hearts are probably lovers of the unlimited. For the welfare of the breed, and the security of descent, they must be held in thorough subjection. Man has captured them and besides providing for and protecting them, it is necessary to keep them "on the chain" as it were. Woe unto him, woe unto them, and woe unto our Race, if ever these lovable creatures should break loose from mastership, and become the rulers or equals of Man. (But that is impossible.) From the earliest ages, Man has captured his wife by force or strategem and to this day he does the same. Marriage ceremonies symbolize his proprietorship—his capture. The marriage ring is one link of a chain, emblematic of the fact that the pre-historic bridegroom chained his "beloved one" in a cave, till she became tame, tractable, reciprocative.

The sexual degeneracy that is now so prevalent among us, is the result of Christian Civilization; that is to say, the Demonetization

---

* *St. James Gazette*, 1896, cablegram from Mashonaland.

of Man and the equalization of women. As long as the husband is absolute Imperator within his own four walls, the poisoning of the marriage bed (now so common, and so loathsome), cannot take place. If his wife or an intruder dares to dishonor him, their death is an effective deterrent. His daughters, controlled with equal vigor, are not permitted to mate with every strumous Dick, Tom and Harry, that comes smirking along, but are "given away" to *men* who are born of Good Stock, or who have proved their inherent manhood and capacity—in carnivorous combat.

In his sexual relations, the insolent interference of Church and State, is gradually reducing Man to a mere cipher, and establishing a system of organized concubinage, or rather promiscuity. The records of our divorce courts show that sexual infidelity is spreading like wildfire. A prominent New Yorker has publicly asserted that two-thirds of the "married" women in that city are systematically unfaithful: and a fat sordid priestling (named Moody) openly advises his female lambs, to enter the joys of 'godly freedom' via that harlot factory, the Divorce Court.

A woman is two-thirds womb. The other third is a network of nerves and sentimentality. To "emancipate" her, is to hand her over to the tender mercies of clerics, who have learned to "play" upon her emotionalism. Then Credos become illegitimately powerful and even dare to dictate "the whole duty of Man." After a time diabolical pastor-theories inspire politics and rule nations. Then the State becomes the individual's Dictator. Men are demonetized while degeneracy and socialistic hybridism sets in, like a slimy flood.

Prostitution (for hire) is also the direct outcome of unnatural conditions, brought about and established by the harmonious infernalism of statesmen and prelates. In many countries this vile thing is 'regulated' by law, and in all great cities it is a sure source of revenue, not only to the police forces, but to every man who invests in real-estate or banking scrip. A great city is a great ulcer, and a great ulcer is a sure sympton of congenital blood poisoning. Undoubtedly the destruction of Sodom and Gommora was a good thing.

If our modern Sodoms were all razed to the ground, how Nature in all her perennial purity would rejoice exultantly? How she would wrap their tombs and crumbling tumuli with a blaze of shining glory.

If the development persists along present lines, the time is not remote when it shall be truthfully recorded: "There is no marriage in America." A terrible menace to manhood lurks in the dictation of Slave Majorities in this as in all other affairs. Under the plausible form of Divorce Proceedings, a devilish enginery has been established: by means of which the once pure Saxon Invaders of North America, are rapidly transforming themselves into hordes of semi-socialistic free-lovers.

The sanctity of the Home is disappearing. No longer can it be asserted that a "man's house is his castle." Marriages are becoming proportionately less and less: and baby-farming by the Government, is in full blast. Home life is withering away under the blight of State Interference and Pastoral Benediction.

Look over at France where (with the growth of government supervision) the absolutism of the husband is attenuated to a mere fiction—and what do you see? A nation steeped in communistic eroticism, as in a stygian sewer. French women are notoriously unfaithful, and the most horrible sexual lusts are practiced and pleasantly laughed at. There promiscuity results in barrenness; and this, when supplemented by correlated self-sterilization, is rapidly transmuting the once all-powerful Frankish Confederacy, into a feeble and decaying tribe of wasted marasma-struck manlings sheltering themselves beneath the all-protecting wing of an Asiatic Despot.

The title of a man to the proprietorship of his wife does not originate with Church, or State, or Majority Votes. It is inherent in the Man himself. It began in capture and is continued by capture, modified of course by mutual affection,* mutual toleration, and parental love. It existed before the State Monstrosity was invented, and it must be maintained intact, even if both Church and State (those twin devils), have to be utterly annihilated. The Christian Church commenced operations among Roman slaves and Syrian harlots. Its founder himself was the fruit of clandestine intercourse. He never married but consorted with publicans, pariahs, magdalenes, all his life. By his silence upon one famous occasion, he condoned adultery; and in his nebulous Paradise (which socialists and anarchists and other priestlings assert will "come" upon earth) he insinuatingly states there is "no marriage or giving in marriage."

During the first three centuries "Christians" was another name for "free lovers"—meeting in catacombs and secret places, to enjoy promiscuous sexualism, before the "end of the world" came—an event they expected every day, for three hundred years.

The leprous repulsiveness of medieval sodalities and modern monasticism, is all too well known, and requires no more than a passing allusion. "The cells where corralled onanism dwells" are as notorious as they are ultra-natural. Not only the lairs of male and female celibates, but the vestries of churches and temples,

---

* 'To nuptial bower he *led* her, blushing like the morn.'

have ever been hot-beds of lasciviousness, seduction, and all uncleanliness.

"The harlot is Christ's sister, and the tramp is Christ's brother;" proclaims "our dear comrade, W.T. Stead," and he ought to know. Has he not theatrically tried his hand at "being a Christ" (vide "Liza Armstrong and Modern Babylon")—in order to turn an honest penny?

In deference to Barbarian prejudices (after the alaric and Atilla immigrations) the Early Church abandoned its communistic Free Loverisms. But to provide holy sanctions and written authority for its change of heart, monkish forgeries of "Epistles from the Saints" were manufactured on an extensive scale and cautiously published throughout Europe.

To-day, with the advent of Triumphant Democracy, all vile old slave-practices are being actively revived.

Verily! Verily! Triumphant Democracy, thou art a foul thing! Triumphant Desolation! Triumphant Amphimixis! Lo! this is the redeeming spirit that was to "cleanse the heathen as white as snow."

Many modern chapels are little better than assignation houses, and the tambourined, uniformed Christlings of the slum-corners are boastfully recruiting from the vilest of the vile. An enterprising Chicago pastor has even started a free-love seraglio (with himself as the divine Thunder Thrower) which he calls 'Heaven,' and one of its ugliest angels has bodily sworn in open Court, that she was impregnated by the Holy Ghost, to whom she bore a son—in the orthodox style.

Altogether primitive Christianity is in its renaissance. Behold it cometh to pass! "Thy kingdom come, Thy will be done, on earth as it is in heaven," is being rapidly and joyously materialized.

Deity hath established Himself as Statute Law. 'The State which is the People' is His throne, and 'the Church which is righteousness' is his footstool. Glory! Glory! Glory! "All the ends of the world hath seen the salvation of *our* God." Behold Christliness realizing itself through social institutionalisms! Behold the golden harvests grown from the seed of Legislation!

O for the Barbarian swarms of the Danube and the Rhine!—for the Blonde Pirates from the Northern Seas! O for men of a spirit, with lion hearts and lion brains!—for one cohort of True Knights, who would consolidate their Hopes and Convictions into Naked Swords! Alas! Alas! Vanity of vanities, all is vanity! The age of Chivalry is dead and gone. "So sleeps the proud of former days—so glory's thrill is o'er."

❋ 3 ❋

In all practical operations, non-principled persons possess a distinctive advantage over "principled" ones. Honesty never succeeds for when it succeeds, it is not honesty. There is no fair play in Love or War, and all life is made up of Love and War. Genuinely honest men, die as a rule like dogs—in a ditch; and in business affairs they are "nowhere." In their dotage or 'in God's good time'—they (nearly always) go over the hill to State Infirmaries, unknown, friendless.

What chance has a conscientious man, when pitted in statesmanship, literature, or commerce, against the Organized Knavery of sanctimonious and powerful cut-throats? To them he is a pigeon to be plucked—a buck to be hunted—a criminal to be chained—a madman to be made sport of—a lamb to be skinned—a heretic to be—burnt alive.

Certainly it is not good strategy for a man to openly proclaim his loss of faith in conventional moralisms: if he desires to get-on in the world. A wiseling keeps his real sentiments on this point to himself—guards them as his own life. The best mask for moral heresy is one of pretended sanctity. It is very effective. Nearly all the Higher Thieves are ostentatiously pious. Thus when you hear pulpiteers and journalists vociferously proclaiming their profound acquiescence in "moral principles," it is safe to conclude that they are engineering some subterranean swindle.

'Belief' is a war-strategem—an instrument of deceit, a convenient falsification formula—a beautiful hoodwink. Hence it is, that very religious and very holy persons, are almost always thorough-going scoundrels at heart—utterly unreliable—utterly untrustworthy. Generally their whole lives are one long drawn out mendacity, and genuineness-of-Thought or Action is in their mind, attenuated to a mere sham.

Politicians, authors, pastors, 'prophets,' historians, philosophers, and editors, are notorious falsifiers of nature and fabricators of subterfuge. Soaked in unnaturalism, saturated through and through with delirium-breeding hasheesh-literature, they become organically incapable of speaking, let alone of thinking or writing honestly. Artificialism has trained them to be prevaricators, and prevaricators they *must* remain until the clods from the grave-digger's shovel rattle down on their coffin lids. As the Old Man of the Mountains trained his fanatical Assassins, and sent them forth to slay, so Civilization trains its Fiendling Intellectuals and sends them forth to assassinate

95

Human Nature. They are the murderers of manliness—the regicides of Thought—the annihilators of heroism. Would that I had a legion of demons, to wring their necks. They have smothered the grand and masterful old Northern *Realisms* beneath pestiferous rubbish-heaps of Oriental Mythology—of Hebrew old clothes. They repeat automatically in sounding diction, what has already been stuffed into them, as it were, with a ramrod. Their learning is the learning of the 'learned pig' in a menagerie; and their virtue is the virtue of a conscientious Jesuit. March of Mind they call it!—'As organs grind the note they're set to...brains jejune...Grind, year in year out, the same Old Tune.'

4

The *men* who conspicuously "succeed in life"—the generals and nobles, merchant-princes, powerful prelates, opulent bankers, wealthy manufacturers, never overload themselves with artificial moral principles. In their secret hearts they utterly despise all evangelisms and as for written law, they are above and beyond its reach. Kings, conquerers, millionaires, are perpetually being denounced for not abiding by Laws and Regulations enacted by Majority Votes.

The man who plays 'the game of life' in strict accord with certain cut and dried principles—principles that everybody knows by heart, is not likely to come out a winner. He who in his younger days, incommodes himself with copy-book moralisms and terror of the Law, is like unto a soldier who (before entering the battlefield) ties his right hand behind his back and pledges himself to strike and shoot his adversaries on one pre-arranged spot of their bodies only. Could such a madman-soldier hope to conquer? What chance would he have if pitted against brave, dauntless, well equipped antagonists, who had not foolishly bound themselves by such a stupid obligation?

"The right of Nature, which writers commonly call *jus naturale,* is the liberty each man hath, to use his own power for the preservation of his own nature: that is to say his own life, and consequently of *doing anything,* which in *his own judgment and reason* he shall conceive to be the aptest means thereto" writes Hobbes in his *Leviathan.* The man who permits himself to be directed and mastered by the insolent moral principles of the Multitude, is like an eagle with clipped wings and broken talons.

In *war,* your chief end is to smash and paralyze your enemy's combinations. To do this effectually you must meet wile with wile, steel with steel, and blow with blow. You must be equally prepared to fight in the open or fight under cover; to fight on sea, to fight on land, to fight in the air. You shall wage your own war—you shall think your own thought. It is pusilanimity that evolves the Slave, and breeds the Idolator. 'Quit yourselves like men, O ye Philistines!'

Tacitus with true Roman stateliness observes: "The gods look with favor upon supreme courage," and Herbert Spencer savagely asserts that "a creature not energetic enough to maintain itself must die." Cursed are the white-livered, they make excellent fertilizer. Truly—'The seed of the wicked shall be cut off.'

This age of ours wants MEN above all things—"men of a spirit"—men ever ready to look into the eyes of death, without winking. Behold! I post up this New Proclaimation. 'The man who made Justice was a Liar.'

Whatever weapon your Enemy possesses, must be duplicated, or improved upon by you. If it suits him to challenge battle in open front, be sure and ambush him in the flank, or straightaway make a hidden detour and charge him in the rear. It is your chief business to delude him, deceive him, decoy him, out-general him, *if you can.* If moral scruples and fear of "what the world will say," prevents you from doing this, then you were born for subordination, and you had better surrender; for you can never hope to vanquish. You *must* be born again.

"Over an open grave" ever lies the road to success. In "the world's broad field of battle," every *man* is a combatant, and to be a successful combatant, he must not only be calculating, cool-headed, and brave but possessed of merciless strategy, a stout heart, a strong arm, and quiet indomitable determination.

Even the Siamese twins waged a life-long civil war. Man, as we have proved, is the King of the Great Carnivores. *Homo, homini lupus.* By heredity and by training, all carnivores are instinctively strategic in their hunt-operations. They lie in wait for their prey, when they cannot capture it by other methods; but they do not hesitate to hunt in the open, if it pleases them to do so. Great animals (whether man or brute) never operate in strict accordance with pre-arranged rules of procedure. If they did so, they could never prosper—and would die of hunger. Their *greatness* lies in springing surprises—in doing exactly what their antagonists (or intended quarry) don't expect them to do—in being beyond and above all moral measurements whatsoever.

Genius in a first class commander is always exemplified, not by his "goodness," but by the originality and aggressive boldness of his pitiless tactics. When he is thought to be in full retreat, he whirls around and annihilates his pursuers. When his adversaries are preparing to give him a hot reception, "he foldeth his tents like the Arabs," and silently wendeth away.

97

When it is whispered he will embattle his defensive legions on the frontiers of the Fatherland, he bridges the Rhine and bounds upon Paris with tooth and claw. When to invaders, he is expected to abandon Moscow and retire, he burns it to the ground, and while his foemen (imbedded in snow and ice) are freezing to death, he shells them with his field batteries. When wiselings predict that he will seize Gaul and establish a Colonial Dictatorship, he fords the Rubicon, marches on Rome and throttles the Law. When his nation's foemen are embattled on Italian plains, he crosses the Punic foam and carries the war into Africa. When he is reported to be assaulting Babylonian Ramparts he digs a new channel for "the River" and writeth "mene mene tekel upharisin" on Balshazaar's walls. When defenders believe he will march up the Slope with drums and banners gay he quietly scales the Heights of Abraham (in the night) and captures Quebec. When western diplomats think he is about to pounce on Constantinople, he runs Baldwin engines through the Great Wall and stuffs the title deeds of the moribund Chinese empire into his overcoat pocket.

5

The man-animal can never be rendered absolutely "moral" because by nature he is as full of wiles as a fox or a Jew. Should he insanely endeavor to abandon his predatory propensities, then he immediately begins to degenerate and ultimately becomes a feeble, diseased, ghost-ridden monstrosity, a horror to look at. Therefore those who conscientiously try to become "honest" and "good" are permitting themselves to be sacrificed—as burnt offerings on Idol Altars.

If *all men* were scrupulously honest, then honesty *might* be all right (although even that is questionable) but if one percent are deliberately dishonest, then it is assuredly all wrong. Under such resultant circumstances the 'ninety and nine' actually become victims of 'the one.' Honest merchants are ruined by dishonest merchants, honest commanders out-maneuvered by dishonest commanders, honest workmen displaced by dishonest workmen, honest judges undermined by dishonest judges, and honest nations reduced to beggary and vassalge by dishonest nations.

Honesty is merely a policy—under given circumstances "the best policy"—nothing more. In all departments of human effort, honesty is used as a cloak for real designs, just as a wood, a ravine, or a stretch of rising ground serves (in campaigning) to hide squadrons deploying for flank movements.

Why then do parents innoculate the plastic minds of their children, with false conceptions of moral conduct, when they themselves must know (from personal experience) that all such conceptions are a positive handicap in the race for Wealth and Power? What a witless procedure, to teach Ideals (at home, at schools, and at college), that we *know* in our hearts are thorough-going Lies, and then expect nobility of personal conduct to be the resultant. Turn out into the world a young man well trained in 'moral principles' and the chances are ninety-nine to one against him.

Indeed the majority of men never win success untill they are middle aged, until they have had time to slough off the false Idealisms, they began the world with. Un-naturalism has never yet bred a race of heroes and never will. All great Races are predatory.

The 'hungry-to-eat-a-man' tiger knows that if he first growls out his intentions, and then openly bounds up to his intended victim, he will (most probably) get an explosive bullet neatly lodged in his cerebrum. Consequently he ambushes himself in the shadow of a rock or behind a log, and leaps upon his 'dinner' with varying results. It is the same—exactly the same, among carnivorous bipeds. A few of them are tigers, hungry-to-eat-a-man, and the rest are—tiger's-meat, hungry to be eaten. The fact is that Civilization's moralisms are wholly ultra-rational, fundamentally un-natural and utterly inoperative. Christian principles and Natural principles mutually antagonize one another. Nature is Anti-Christ. Darwinism is the mortal foe of Hebraism.

Nature's command is, "Be egoistic, possess the earth and fight it out." Jesus insists, "Be altruistic, abandon the world, and love your enemies." Darwin proclaims, 'All ye are rival carnivores! Be strong therefore, and bold, and fear—Nothing.' Christ teaches, "All ye are dearly beloved brethren. Be obedient therefore and 'good' and fear—Ghosts." Jesus urges his devotees to *pray* for deliverance. Darwin gently intimates his heartfelt belief in the Law of Battle. 'He who will not *work*, neither shall he eat' is the Apostolic pronunciamento. "He who will not fight, neither can he eat" is Nature's savage logic.

'It is more blest to give than to receive' is the vacuous baby-prattle of the Pastor. It is more blest to *capture* than to receive, is ordinary Common Sense.

He who denies man's right to exploit man, impeaches, not the conduct of man, but the order of natufe.

Who then is right—the Anglo-Saxon or the Israelite? The scientist or the oratorical wonder-worker? The Western thinker or the Eastern dreamer? Which is the True Faith: Japhet's logic or Shem's Fabulism?

99

6

Common-sense provides no precise solution of Right or Wrong. "All moral philosphy is false and vain" for *man* is unlimited. In the realm of Ethics, most modern wiselings are fanatical and unreasonable bigots. They really believe that Ethical Principles are as a house built upon a rock; whereas "the House" is an unfounded hypothesis, and "the Rock" non existent.

Good and Evil liveth only in men's minds. They are not Realities but shadows—credos—ghosts—and only the maddest of the mad worship their own Shade.

What is Right—what is Wrong? These elemental interrogatories have been asked in every age, and every age formulates replies to suit itself. *De facto* Right and Wrong are no more than arbitrary algebraic signs, representing hypnagogic phantasies. They are mere symbols emblematic of belated fragments of insolent ecclessiastical crudities. In nature, all developments are essentially *one* and the same phenomenon infinitely transfused and intermingled. Good and Evil are human inventions, born of human foolery, narrowness, and short-sightedness. The organic brain is far too small and too contemptible, to *completely* comprehend what nature is driving at. What appears to be wrong to us, may be right in nature, and vice versa.

We can no more establish an infallible system of ethics, than we can establish infallible systems of religion, philosophy or politics. All the Universe is in a state of flux, and men are but a swarm of querulous, heat-evolved insectivores, living aimlessly on the top of a floating cork, that whirls and darts and rolls over and over and over, amid the scum and froth and slime of a boiling, bubbling Alembic. Within his own sphere individual man is, and ought to be, the supreme determinant. Outside of that sphere he knows absolutely nothing—and philosophy *less than nothing.*

As for the prophets of Futurity, from the days of Guatama, Bel, and Ishtar, down to Christ, Mahomet, Peter, Luther, Calvin, and Brigham Young, they have been strident "deceivers all" working on the emotional credulity of women—and doltish rabbles. A false teacher may be earnestly and honorably sincere in all his theoria, but that does not necessarily deomonstrate intrinsic divinity. Many false prophets have been murdered (because of their opinions) besides Jesus of Nazareth, Judea, and Smith of Nauvoo, Illinois. The execution of the founder of Mormonism (inspired by political clamor) is an exact parallel to the execution of the founder of Christianity (inspired by priestly clamor). The point is—neither shooting nor crucifixion are satisfactory proofs of divinity or probity.

Right and Wrong, like Up and Down, East and West, are relative terms, without any fixed or finite meaning. What is good for the goose is *not always* good for the gander. Newfoundland lies East from Chicago, but West from Berlin. All depends upon the point of view. Consequently what may be 'right' in one age may, in another age, be wholly 'wrong.'

In ancient Rome it was considered the height of impiety, heresy, and treason, for free born citizens to adore a circumcised Asiatic; but in modern Europe and America, it is considered pious and fashionable and highly commendable to do so.

Even what is right to one man, under one set of circumstances, may be utterly wrong to the same man under a different set of circumstances. Cromwell as colonel of the Ironsides, thought regal absolutism the essence of all diabolism: but as President of the Reublic, he defended it (in himself) as—'a crowning mercy.'

When Government soldiers shoot down American "rebels" that is called "a glorious victory," but when Government soldiers shot Colonial rebels during the Red Flag Riots (inaugural of the War of Independence) that is conventionally labelled 'wicked massacre.'

When a band of rich men plunder the poor, that is business shrewdness, practical statesmanship, or financial integrity; but if bands of poor men plunder the rich, that is larceny, burglary, highway robbery, and rebellion. When the Anglo-Saxon invader is cooped-up and slaughtered in India, that is mutiny and red-handed murder; but when *he* mows down the sepoys in battalions, or fastens them to the muzzles of cannon and blows them into ribbons, that is upholding the majesty of Law and of Order. When Cuban guerrillas kill Spaniards, all American papers describe it as "war" but when the Spaniards retaliate and kill the Cubans, that is 'horrible butcheries by General Weyler.' Spanish cut-throats are glorified (in Spain) as dashing heros, and the Cuban patriots described as brigands, outlaws, and brutal Negro murderers. *All depends upon the point of view.*

Victory sanctifies. In the realm of abstract Ethics there is no other Fact upon which the plain man can finally make up his mind. As far as Sociology is concerned, ethical principles are decided by the shock of contending armies. Right has always been emblazoned on the standards of Victory, and wrong on the draggled rags of Lost Causes.

When Brennus, commander of the ancient Gauls, attacked the Clusians a Roman ambassador protested, asking "what offense have the Clusians given you?" Brennus laughed at the question, and replied: "Their offense is the refusal they make to divide the country with me. It is the same offense that the people of Alba, the Fidenians and Ardeans gave you: and lately the Vienians, the Falisci, and the Volsci. To avenge yourselves, you took up arms and washed your injury in their blood: you subdued the people, pillaged their houses, and laid waste their cities and their countries: and in this you did no wrong or injustice: you obeyed the most ancient laws, which gave to the Strong the possessions of the Weak; the sovereign law of nature, that begins with the gods and ends with the animals. Suppress therefore O Romans, your pity for the Clusians. Compassion is yet unknown to the Gauls: do not inspire them with that sentiment, lest they should have compassion upon those you oppress."

History is full of similar logic. Brutus, for instance, who poinarded Julius Ceaser (his friend and benefactor), has always been held up to public estimation as "the noblest Roman of them all," whereas Booth, who slew Abraham Lincoln, is everywhere and at all times, spoken of as a malevolent assassin.

The operation of the 'Law' itself, is also apt illustration of the paradoxical nature of Right and Wrong. Citizens who break the written law are hailed before judges, inquisatorially cross-examined, and chained for long years in State dungeons: but the statesmen and legislators may sell their country for gold, and break every statute law and constitution in the land; without the least fear of legal intimidation. Indeed the approbation of the State, is all-sufficient nowadays to sanctify any crime—even the most abominable. In this particular (of granting absolution) the State is gradually supplanting and absorbing the Church.

(The *Protestors* of the past demolished the infallible imperialism of clericals over religio-individual thought; and the Protestantism of the future must demolish the insolent dictatorship of Politicals over private judgment, and the development of Personality.)

All 'good Christian men' regard the judicial murder of Jesus as a crime of the blackest dye, but they chant church-paeans of joy over Jael's murder of Sisera, and the assassination of Eglon King of Moab, etc. It is not very long ago since Catholic and Protestant idolators, mutually roasted each other alive "for the glory of God and the uplifting of his Holy Name." Each side proclaimed themselves right, with rack and thumbscrew, and other little instruments of persuasion. Protestants still think it a crime and a scandal to worship the mother of their God, but Catholics consider it right and proper to deify the Hebrew maid, who remained a maid (what a paradox?) after borning a son.

To eat pork and beans is frightfully wicked for a Jew, but passable for a cultured Bostonian. To drink whiskey is iniquity to a Turk, but exhilirating to a Scotlander. Roast beef is a goodly dish

102

to an English 'barbarian,' but famine-striken orthodox Hindoos die rather than taste thereof. Duelling is honorable in some countries but dishonorable in others. So are pugilism, private revenge, tyrannicide, bull-fighting, regicide, and warfare. The Quakers, Anarchists, and Young Men's Christian Associations, are unceasingly railing against 'war and all its horrors,' whereas there are not a few benighted infidels (including the author), who regard war as nature's Greatest Prophylactic.

Polygamy is "wrong" in England and America, but monogamy is righteousness, and polyandry "right" (being licensed by the State); whereas in Europe and among all "savage" tribes, polyandry is iniquity, polygamy—blessedness, and monogamy—vileness.

In ancient Lacedaemon stealing was considered highly meritorious *if not found out*, as in modern America. Solon places theft among the professions, and he knew what he was doing. Aristotle includes 'robbery' among the different kinds of hunting. (There was no hypocrisy about these classical authors. They called a spade a spade, and searched Nature (not libraries) for facts. Herein is the secret of their genius and undying renown.) If a man steals a horse or a steer, he is lynched (if captured) as an 'enemy of society' but if he steals the value of a million horses by wrecking a savings bank, he is straightway made a Senator or Knighted. It is a criminal act to burglarize another man's house, but it's "enlarging our markets" to steal Texas from the Mexicans; Alsace and Lorainne from the French; Egypt from the Turks; or Madagascar from the Hovas. The fact is, that, all the greatest statesmen and kings have been (most commendably) the Higher Criminals. Wars are marauding expeditions and all kingship and property originates in Warfare.

Slay one man (in order to rob him) and you are a murderer. Slay a million men (in order to rob them) and you are a renowned general. Annex from *one* person and you are a felonious ruffian, but annex from *the whole population*, or from rival nations, and you are made Chancellor of the Exchequer; Chairman of Ways and Means; or decorated with the grand cross of the Legion of Honor. Maraud direct for your own profit, and you are a heinous rascal, counterfeiter, forger, bandit; but maraud indirect, 'on public service only' and you are proclaimed "our opulent fellow-citizen and distinguished patriot."

Take from the peasantry even an infinitesimal proportion of their petty property, and they will lynch you as a lazy thievish tramp; but *take* two-thirds of their harvests by law and rule (rent, interest or tax assessments) and they will turn out in the middle of the night, to cheer you in your steam-horsed palace car, as it whirls through their 'God forsaken' villages.

To "steal the goose from off the common" is awful rascality, but "to steal the common from the goose" is splendid statesmanship. Men who write down Holy Fables in books are called Apostles of God, or canonized as saints; but men who tell regulation lies in the ordinary course of business are popularly supposed to be wicked and ungodly scamps. The delightful storyteller who prints a pleasing yarn, coined out of his alcholic imagination, is known as a gifted author: but the plain blunt writer who interprets Facts and proclaims them openly, is an incarnation of iniquity, madness, blasphemy—a veritable Apollyon, Satan. "What is one man's meat is another man's poison."

Again, he who prevaricates in a pulpit for 'the Glory of God' is everywhere known as a Doctor of Divinity, but he who bears false witness in an ordinary Court of Justice, is universally condemned as a perjured villain.

It is questionable if there is one codified crime that would be considered a crime in every land on earth. Just as there are a thousand different icons and ideals of god, so there are a thousand mutually repellant views of Right and Wrong. Every climate, every nation, every community, has its own notion of what Virtue means. Moral Dogmas are *manufactured* to suit the occasion, and are always used as instruments of intimidation. They are not necessarily in harmony with, or based upon Nature: except in the sense that Fraud is natural. Biologically and historically considered—'there is nothing either Right or Wrong, but *thinking* makes it so.'

Every age and nation must interpret Right and Wrong for itself. *So must every man.* It is each man's manifest duty to invent his own Ethical Credo. If he neglects this duty, and supinely (without thinking) adopts the Credo of the herd into which he is born, then his individuality is merged and lost. Other men with more personal will-power, may then set up fallacious, maladroit Dogmas—counterfeit twenty-four inch guages—and compel him to "conform" against his wish. They become rulers and proprietors, while he descends to the position of a dependent or vassal. Here is the permanent menace to freedom that lies imbedded in all ethical, political, and religious Codes.

He who "keeps the commandments" of another, is necessarily the servant of that other. He who curbs his own thought, to please a majority, has already lost his mental liberty. He who implicitly relies upon "public opinion" becomes a mere marionette—a bloodless dummy. Professing independence, he is practically a prisoner in his own domain.

The pride of life is in *deciding* and *doing*—in *taking the initiative*—not in obeying the dictation of others. He who "keeps the commandments" is, and must always remain a subordinate—in a beggardom of rules and regulations. He who disobeys "the commandments" becomes himself a Commandment-Maker; that is to say, a ruler over the minds and bodies and property of inferior organisms. Obedience is characteristic of the menial. Disobedience is the stamp of the hero. "Man is the measure of all things."—*(Protagoras)*

"He who takes no initiative, and determines no issues, however intelligent and trustworthy: plays a subordinate part."* All great deeds are the result, not of Majority Votes, but of Individual Activity.

Every man who is free (and freedom means something more than the mere privilege of dropping regulation pieces of print into a Majority Box) should judge 'all things' by his own personality. He should regard himself as the measuring rod—the determinant—the unit of value, and carefully abstain from blindly adopting other men's measurements, without personal verification and reasonable tests.

The easiest way for a band of public robbers to plunder a nation, is for them to *issue counterfeit currency, and exchange it for intrinsic values:* and the easiest way to enslave a Race is to wheedle it into, or impose upon it counterfeit Ethics, that is to say, fraudulent standards of morality.

When the weighing scales (or measures) are falsified, all subsequent exchange becomes marauding. Then foreclosing bankers become cattle-lifters, and machine politicians develop into pirates. Thus it happeneth that the words 'politician' and 'thief' are *now* interchangeable terms; more especially in America, France, and Australia. "Government *is* the Great Blackmailer."

🦋 7 🦋

Better far, for a free animal to be killed outright, than to be mastered, subordinated, and enchained.

Mentally, morally, physically, a full-grown man should swear allegiance to no extraneous moralism, custom, or arbitrary rule-of-conduct. He ought to take a special pride in developing his own individuality; independent of all other men whatsoever. In the maxim "union is strength" there lies an abiding fallacy. Very often, in practical affairs, he is greatest who stands most apart. "Every man for himself" is the law of life. Every man for an Institution, a God, or a Dogma, is the law of death. "Mind your own business" is a line of thought very much neglected in this infirm

---

* Admiral Walker, U.S.N., in *Forum*, Dec., 1896.

age; when every sodden degenerate fancies that it is his "business" to be every other degenerate's keeper, guardian and nurse. Cain's wrathful retort "am I my brother's keeper?" contains a far reaching practical philosophy, that is deserving of calm consideration, in the light of contemporary socialistic maladjustments and biologic evolutionism. Only the terrorized repent, but non-moralists found families, build cities, rule the earth and laugh at the Gods.

Each individual should think as he pleases—as "the spirit moves him"—without the least respect for what others think or do—the only limit to his actions being (of course) the materialized opposition he actually meets with: for the Strong are the natural limit of the Strong. No one is bound to obey another (or a majority) *except* "the other" can coerce obedience; and to do that at all times, under all circumstances, would be terribly troublesome, expensive, and—dangerous.

When actualized antagonism is met with, it is every dauntless man's business to surmount it—if he can. Should he find that beyond his strength (or the massed power of his friends and supporters), then death or submission are the only reasonable alternatives. If he has not the nerve to fall (as the much maligned Catiline fell at Pistoria*), then he and his posterity to the third and fourth generation must sink to subjectivity.

If he is coerced by superior Strength (or strategy) into temporary retreat; he then owes no allegiance whatever to his triumphant adversaries: and he should be ever ready (when time and tide seem propitiatory) to overwhelm and destroy their dictation. 'Get there!' I say, get there!—Get there at any cost!

Be *you* a True Knight. Save thyself by thine own high deeds. If a man wound you on one cheek, lay him low—smite him hip and thigh. Self preservation is the first law of thy being. Hate for hate, and ruth for ruth—scorn for scorn and tooth for tooth. Get there, I say!—Get there! Get there at any cost!

Let him no longer boast of his bravery who merely weeps with his Dear-Ones, when his Dear-Ones weep for bread. The gallant and the brave, have never yet been known to want for *anything*. Women shed tears; men shed—blood. Cowards serve masters. Bold men make themselves Masters.

When passing through the Valley of Humiliation, slaves and dastards, exposing their sores, sob aloud for consolation and sympathy. Brave men stand apart and ponder vengeance or conquest.

---

* "All wounded in front; not a man taken alive: Catiline himself gasping out his life, ringed round with corpses of his foemen."—*Sallust*

The fear of death is the beginning of Slavery. Majority-Box despotism can only be maintained, by making a sudden and violent death its final sanction. "Civilized" men are terrorized at the idea of death, and as long as that is so, those who wield sudden death in the hollow of their hand, are masters of the world. Hence a small body of disciplined fighters (if protected by the death penalty) are capable of dominating a nation of ten thousand times their number.

Hence also, in accordance with the "fight-fire-with-fire" principle, all secret associations aiming at the destruction of established tyrannies, in Church or State, have ever been organized (from the most ancient times) upon a "death penalty" basis. When successful, these societies become "Government" in their turn; merely re-forming as *defense* forces instead of *aggressive* forces. On this account the inner workings of 'government' are unknown to the outer world.

Every ministerial Cabinet is oath-bound and all the higher officials are pledged and obligated under a death penalty, to the most strict secrecy. Indeed under the cover of Popular Government, the Financial Empire of the World is an established Fact.

No man has (or ever had) any *inherent* right to the use of the earth; nor to personal independence; nor to property, nor wives, nor to liberty of speech; nor to freedom of thought; nor to *anything* except he can (by himself or in conjunction with his allies) assert his "rights" by Power. What are (in popular parlance) called "rights," are really "spoil"—the prerogatives of formerly exerted Might: but a "right" lapses immediately, when those who are enjoying it, become incapable of further maintaining it. Consequently all "rights" are as transient as morning rainbows, international treaties, or clauses in a temporary armistice. They may be abrogated at any moment, by any one of the contracting parties, holding the necessary Power.

Broadly speaking therefore, Might is incarnated Right, and rights are metaphorical mights. Power and Justice are synonyms; for Might is mighty and *does* prevail. They who possess the *undisputable* Might (be they one, ten, or ten million) may and *do* proclaim the Right. Government is founded on property, property is founded on conquest, and conquest is founded on Power—and Power is founded on brain and brawn—on Organic Animality. Just as parents dictate right to their children, so masterful animals dictate right to millions and millions of sodden-livered, baby-minded men. Monarchic rulers are the gaudy jumping-jacks, and representative institutions the tax-gathering mechanism of the Mighty-Ones. Banks and safe-deposits are their treasure-stores, and armies and navies their sentinels, executioners, watchmen.

"There is much to be said for the opinion," writes Professor Huxley, "that Force effectually and thoroughly used, so as to render further opposition useless; establishes an ownership that *should be recognized as soon as possible.*" Professor Jevons expresses a parallel thought: "The first step must be, to rid our minds of the idea that there are such things as abstract rights." "Spiritual right" and "moral right" cannot possibly be explained, because they are merely verbalisms without solid substance. They are not even shadows, for a shadow implies a materialized actuality. It is somewhat difficult to define what is non-existent. That task may be left to University professors and Sunday school divines. They are adepts at clothing their mental nudity in clouds of wondrous verbosity.

Right, in its broadest and deepest sense can be logically defined however, as the manifestations of solar energy, materialized through human thought and thew, upon Battlefields—that is to say, in Nature's Supreme Court. Might is victory and victory establishes rightness. Might is cosmic power in chemic operation; and Man (in his own sphere) is heliocentric force on two legs. Might is mighty and *must* prevail.

It *does* prevail, for verily it is as the Law of Gravitation—Nay!—*it IS the law of gravitation.*

All arbitrary rules of Right and Wrong are insolent invasions of personal liberty. He who would maintain his manhood, must ignore them and abandon them, wherever and whenever possible; *except* he has investigated them—paralleled them with Nature, and without coercion agrees to abide thereby as a modus-vivendi. If he accepts them (on other conditions) as his life-long load, that is—his funeral. If he is eager to handicap himself or commit suicide, why shouldn't he? That's *his* own business.

A sensible man should never conform to any rule or custom, simply because it has been highly commended by others, alive or dead. If they are alive he should suspect their motives. If dead they are out of Court. He should be a law unto himself in all things; otherwise he permits himself to be demonetized to the level of a domesticated animal.

The real man must depend upon himself absolutely, determine his own ends, decide his own plan of campaign; and savagely resent any authoritarian interference (especially if it takes the form of socialistic officialism). He must be resolutely on his defense, against all those meddlesome "dogs" who dare to impose their squalid ideals upon his private or public life.

It would be well for him also to be a thorough-going and dangerous adversary, as well as an unswerving friend. To his foemen he should be as pitiless as 'the gods'; to his friends in all days of difficulty and danger, he should be, as—'an army with banners.'

Therefore I say be manly!—be *both* manly and wise! Be fearless, tenacious, resolute, and bold; for (as Von Clausewitz sagaciously insists), "boldness, directed by an overruling intelligence is the brand of the hero."

A man's *first* duty in this world is to *himself,* and the word 'himself' includes those near and dear ones, who have twined their tendrils around his heart. A man's kindred are part of himself. He should not forget that when fighting for his own hand, he is fighting for them. His strength is their rampart. Their strength is his glory. The family and the individual are a unit.

Henry Watterson, an insolent editor of the New Dispensation, in a studied oration before the Wall St. Board of Trade, thus brazenly re-voices the divine-right of Communalism over the fates of men: "We are to teach the lesson that the citizen exists for the government, not the government for the citizen." Ignatius Loyolas; Calvins, Duke of Alvas; Torquemadas; and Piuses by the score; have been equally eloquent in expounding parallel diobolical sophisms. For ages those Destroyers of Liberty proclaimed that the individual existed for the Holy Church; not the Holy Church for the individual. However the despotism of socialistic-sacredotalism has been thoroughly tamed—blown to fragments as it were; and the right of private judgment fully maintained. Its cunning recrudescence under the guise of State Infallibility, by the Jesuits of journalistic Diablerie must be met as resolutely, and smashed as savagely, relentlessly, as its informal theoretic prototype. The majesty of the Individual first, foremost, and above all things. "Hell's blazes" are realized among us, when "the individual withers and the State grows more and more."

Should the Wattersonian ideal triumph, every man who *then* dares to open his mouth (except to extol Authority) will run the risk of having streams of lead pumped into it, as a gentle hint to be constitutional.

He who acts upon self-denial principles in his dealings with rival carnivores casts himself down that they may climb over his prostrate personality to *their success.* He abdicates his inherent royalty who bends before any human being or any human dogma—but his own. Humbleness is a crime in a man, though it may be a virtue in a menial. The 'modest' man permits his rivals to occupy all the High Places and make him their footstool—nay, their very doormat.

Of course there are certain Higher Laws, which no one can even *try* to rebel against, without being quietly executed. The transgressor of a natural Ordinance may think he has escaped, even while the noose-knot is under his chin and the bolt about to be sprung. Nature has a very long arm and a vengeful one. Many a "city of the plain" has been incinerated, besides Sodom and Gomorrah. Individual transgressors of nature are always driven mad: and nations that organize defiance to the nature of their being: become regimented hordes of incoherent manlings, sootily prespiring downward to their "heaven" dancing the dance of death, shrieking the songs of 'Progress.' Observe for example the working classes of civilization and the utter lunacy of their doings. Undoubtedly their god has struck them blind or mayhap they are 'possessed of a devil.' Certainly they are not sane. The day is near at hand when they shall cry out with shame "O, would that we were dead!"

As rapidly as machinery can be perfected, to perform the work now being done by these animals; they are being "dispensed with"—turned adrift in hordes to find fodder and shelter as best they can. Hired-men are rapidly becoming cheaper than horses and dogs, but as yet somewhat dearer than electric motors and steam engines. The average workman therefore feels instinctively that his 'virtues' may not, after all, preserve his throat from the knife—that is to say, from the logical consequences of his own, or his forefathers' defeat in the struggle. His "virtues" (as he calls them, poor devil) are extreme laboriousness, extreme docility, extreme political and religious credulity—together with extreme pusilanimity in his own defense. As long as Power requires these hordes of slave-hirelings, they will be provided with enough necessaries to keep themselves in proper trim; but when their Labor Force is no longer a profitable investment, they will assuredly be eliminated.* Why should prisoners of war be kept alive anyhow at vast expense; when it becomes cheaper and more convenient, to turn them adrift—to perish as valueless stock perish on the ranges in winter time? Already many of these "freeborn citizens" are cutting their throats daily in despair, at being unable to find a master. Millions are also slowly drugging themselves with succulent poisons, in the shape of alcoholic and other stimulants. Scientific sterilization is an established custom;

---

* "The muzzles of the repeating rifles pointing at their heads, had a quieting effect on the miners." *Daily Paper*

infanticide a regular trade; and celibacy increasing by leaps and bounds. The fact is that the industrial world is run on business principles, and 'business principles' are a synonym for 'woe to the vanquished,' 'hell takes the hindmost,' 'the survival of the fittest' and 'might is right.'

Right, like water, finds its own level. Man's consent is not necessary to the operation of Natural Forces. It is not required. It is not even asked. He is like unto a patient strapped firmly upon a dissecting table. He may feel the surgeons lance sinking through his quivering flesh—he may shiver in terror and break out into a cold sweat—he may groan in convulsive agony and pray to his Idol—but, he cannot escape.

Knowing all this, why not let Nature alone to work out her own silent ends? Why should communities of creeping-things try to safe-guard their incapables? Why obstruct the drastic and significant removal of corrupted organisms? The Jesus type of men were clearly made to be crucified and flogged. The Buddha type were (evidently) born to die of pestilence and famine—poor weak cowardly swarms of rotting vermin that they are! Behold them in the distance there, with their ribs sticking through their hides, accepting with doleful thankfulness the alms of their Conquerers.

Brahma! Brahma! Confucious! Juggernaut! Christ!—Behold— Your glorious handiwork!

Let the cowardly and the vile die off—let them annihilate themselves: that is the logic of the spheres. The atmosphere of this terrestrial ball will be purer, when these "heavy laden souls" are gone, and there will be elbow room upon its surface, for the regeneration of Purity and Cleanliness of mind and body.

At the banquet of life, let no seat be reserved for those who cannot win it—who cannot *break into* the enchanted circle, by force of character and force of deeds. The impotent and the brainless, who call themselves "the righteous" are better dead anyhow—better for themselves, and better for their successors. Is it not the height of madness, for communities to deliberately nourish and foster, the bacteria of hereditary degeneration?

Superiority can only be decided by Battle. Conflict is an infallible method of Selection and Rejection. Evolution has no end. That is undoubtedly, the logical deduction of Darwin's famous pronouncement: "If he (man) is to advance still higher, it is to be feared that he must remain subject to a severe struggle. Otherwise he would sink into indolence; and the more gifted men would not be more successful than the less gifted."

It is only Incoherents of subjective will-power or of servile extraction (bottle-fed beings as it were) that even dream of an "ordered state of society" wherein Right and Wrong (or personal merit) can be decisively decided upon by other than biological principles.

Hebrew decadents harped upon this fool-thought of Universal Peace, Equality, Justice, and Fair Play for ages: but have they not been a pestilent tribe of unwarlike slaves from their leprous beginning? The greatest poem of their repulsive literature, inculcates the "virtue" of patience and submission under intolerable Injustice. All their gyrating prophets scream, and sob, and yell over the wholesale failure of epileptoid ethical standards; and insanely proclaim a 'good' time coming; when every Israelite "shall recline under his own vine and fig tree, with no one to make him afraid." How delightful? Moses, Jesus, Isaiah, Peter—Mark, Matthew, Luke and John, were all squalid Jews, and rhapsodical Communards. Those Hebrew breeders of desolation—Lasalle, Dr. Adler, Jacobi, Karl Marx, are modernized transplanted Essenes—Ebionites.

All moral injunctions, all millenialisms; are arbitrary infernalisms—the results of crafty hypnotic suggestion. Their secret object is the overthrow of human reason and individual independence; in order to establish a vast bedlamite penitentiary to be called 'God's kingdom on earth' alias 'pandemonium in full blast.'

The fact is, Humanity is going stark raving mad in consequence of having eaten the fruit that grows on that devilish tree "the tree of the knowledge of good and evil." Luscious it is to look upon—pleasant it is to the palate, but a deadly atrophine—a cunning poison lurks in its core. Cursed are they who eat thereof.

Aye, thrice cursed are the *believers* in Right and Wrong—for they *are*—the erring ones.

🐦 9 🐦

Attraction and gravitation hold the stars in their courses and (upon exactly the same general operative method) all human swarms and animal herds, are integrated and disintegrated by effective manifestations of derivative solar heat and power.

Strong-Men are magnetized incarnations of primordial energy—dynamos of concentrated electricity. There is a mysterious, almost magical charm about the personality of True Greatness. Lesser men are attracted to their Natural Chiefs as steel shavings are drawn to the loadstone. This peculiar attractive force is hardly ever seen (except spasmodically) in physical weaklings. It seems to develop only in animals of unusual vitality—men with plenty of "devil" in them.

112

Physical power is the basis of mental power. The nutriment of the brain cells is derived from the blood-corpuscles perpetually being pumped into it by the heart's action. If the pump valves are weak or out of gear—if the food stream is impure—if the stomach is disordered—if the liver is congested or the lungs decaying and corrupt; then the brain is starved, drugged, poisoned, while all the thoughts that germinate therein are feeble, unnatural, impure. Hence the rolling stream of literary filth that the Zolas' and the bible-boomers, the poetlings, and the 'eminent savants,' keep pouring out upon generations of men, soaked ages in similar intellectual sewerage.

Hence also the remarkable fact, that neither Great Men *nor* Great Heroisms are ever town bred. Cities are impure in thought, word and deed; and nothing that is noble can ever evolve therein. They are the refuse heaps—the kjokken-moddings of the world. They are matrixes of all that is shameful and base, in religion, politics, sociology, and law. Lupanars of organized abomination are they!—where the infamous prostitute and the still more infamous editor poison the air, side by side; spreading abroad their leprous contagion with every wind that blows. Would that I were a Nero and could play the fiddle! But after all perhaps, it would be a waste of matches and good cat-gut.

Great men can only evolve from out an environment of comparative personal independence. They come from the mountains and the forest clearings. They grow to maturity with the storm beating upon, and the rains dripping adown them. First, warring against the rivalry of the elements, they develop the tremendous motor-power necessary in after life, for the mastership of man-herds. Entering into the centers of semi-morbibund civilizations, they straightaway take the lead as a matter of natural right. They become rulers, chancellors, kings, conquerers, electric batteries, dynamos. Slave-bred swarms toil at their bidding, with zealous contentment and rivals are cast down, as it were, by a "turn of the wrist."

Their smile is wealth and honor to lesser-men—their frown is poverty, outlawry, or the bow-string. Second-class animals gather around them, and are used up as satraps, governors, lieutenants. If a nation under process of exploitation, revolts, the revolt is supressed by *force.* If established rulers are incapable of that task, then are they overthrown; and leaders of Revolt rule in their stead—as a matter of course. Rulers' control depends absolutely upon their Might. When unable any longer to wield the "death penalty," their power is departed. The French aristocracy originated in the savage deeds of fierce, long-haired, battle-bred Franks; and their effeminate descendents—were overwhelmed and guillotined by Grim Provincials who came to Paris, hungry for money, power and renown.

In the regions of stellar Space similar phenomena may be noted. That sun-star with the strongest attractive power, whirls other and lesser stars around it until finally it comes in contact with a rival rolling mass of greater magnitude and attractiveness, whereupon it is absorbed and loses its individuality. What the law of gravitation is to matter and motion, the law of Might is in the province of sociology. In this analogy there is illimitable significance embedded.

Star life is known to be an emanation of primeval plutonic energy. Our planetary system is like unto one whirling mote (among countless myriads) in a vitalized sunbeam. Our earth is a by-product of secondary cyclonic rage. The sun itself (the power-house of *our* world) is materialized heat-force in active operation; manifesting itself as warmth, light, motion, electricity, and animal life.

Man's body and sustenance is derived, directly or indirectly from the Sun. By it he lives, dies, and has his being. Let heliocentric force be withdrawn for an instant, and all life straightway disappears. Thus everywhere, throughout "Eternity," under all circumstances and at all times, this world, all worlds, and all that creeps thereon are driven, inspired, vitalized, and guided by active operating Force. Everywhere it is Might that governs, feebleness that is governed, attracted, repelled, controlled.

Force propels iron-ribbed reindeers of the sea and hurls them plunging through the gray-green surges. Force whirls the loaded freight cars over prairie, range, and river. Force hauls-up from the deep sunk mines, vast treasures of gold, iron, silver and coal. Force rolls the red-glowing metal ingots into titanic shapes. Force sows the seed, plows the field, reaps the grain, threshes the corn, hews the stone, shapes the girders, bridges rivers, mows down forests, builds cities, writes the book—inspires it, prints it, defends it.

Even "the music of the spheres" is the vibrant roar of warring elementals, chanting the Gloria of Power.

If Force is the "all in all" of the planetary systems and the animal world, may it not also be the open-sesame of sociology—the primeval principle that governs (and must continue to govern) the relations of tribe to tribe and man to man? Is it not the gospel of antiquity, as well as the logical reducto of To-day?

Whether in mortgaged republics, pawned monarchies, or hypothecated despotisms, the Sword Power—(that is to say, the military power—the clubbing power) is the ultimate *ipse dixit* in the measuring-out of right and wrong. As it was in the days of the fierce Sesostris, the devastating Ghengis, the venturesome Charlamagne, so is it even now. In all industrial relations Might is 'monarch of all it surveys.' Authority is Authority, though it may take on a thousand diverse forms. What is the elemental difference between a Roman mandamus, a Turkish firman, a Russian ukase, a 'Supreme' Court injunction, or an Order in Chancery? They are exact synonyms. Whatever their salient phraseology may be, in operation they are visible manifestations of Imperial Power—of Sceptered Majesty. No sacredotal sophistry can permanently disguise this fact; and what is more important, no emotional demagoguery can remove it.

Authority is not an evil in itself. It is as natural for men of Power to rule Feeble multitudes, as it is for the lion to eat the lamb. When any nation, or class of men possess no real might, it is just and proper that they should be subordinated: and again, if they develop the requisite strength, it is equally justifiable for them to reconquer their former position; and subordinate their subordinators. Evolution works through Authority but there is to it no limitation.

The penalty of defeat is tremendous. Wage-earning is (in modern times) the main clause in the treaty under which the defeated are permitted to exist.

Even-handed Justice has never existed in the animate creation and never can. The very idea of it is an absurdity. Evolution knows it not.

Between beasts of burden and beasts of prey; also between Capital and Labor there is an eternal combat. Natural enemies are they of each other, and whichever proves the stronger must rule— for the time being; or rather, until the next Test. The law of battle is unlimited. It does not end to-day or to-morrow. It persists for all time.

Between the Optimates and Populares of Rome—the Aristos and Helots of Greece—the Merchant-Kings and Nubian serfs of Carthage—the Military Caste and the slaves of Karnack and Memphis, the same irrepressible conflict raged for long centuries that is now being waged *everywhere*, between the Haves and the Have-nots. Indeed the agrarian agitation, and the tumultuous strife between the Debtor and the Creditor classes in modern America, is an exact duplicate of what happened in the Graeco-Roman world. Modern leaders, however, (on both sides) are poor miserable weaklings, compared with the chiefs of Antiquity. Mere infants are they, delighting in toys and lullabies—seeing, they see not; hearing, they hear not; minds they have, but they know not; laughing and prattling they *say* naught—most eloquently. To them their petty provincial cradle is the Universe, and their lives an aimless wandering in the land o' dreams.

The men who talk of permanently reconciling conflicting world-wide energies, are wasting their breath for naught. Compromise is out of the question (now as of old) except as a temporary expedient. The rich and the poor are both inevitable natural products and complements of each other—like the opposing currents in an electric battery. It is the business of the rich to exploit the poor and it is equally the business of the poor to defeat and exploit—in their turn.

The oppression of one class by another is always induced by the physical cowardice of the victimized; and Nature has no love for dastards—whether rich or poor. Oppression is one of the *necessary* phases of evolution. In order therefore to insure the subordination and ultimate annihilation of lower types; the struggle for survival is imposed upon humans as upon all other animals. Even when our 'eminent' wiselings are predicting eras of universal peace and contentment, the contending cohorts are preparing to jump at each other's throats—as of yore. Might must decide 'all things' in the future, as it has decided 'all things' in the past: and they who teach otherwise, are either dishonest or have no real conception of the magnitude and sequence of biological determinance.

'All the world' is now in Debt and no human effort can ever suffice to repay the interest (let alone the principal) in cash. Business lives under a cloud of mortgage indebtedness, that must someday be liquidated with shot and shell, for bonds infer—bondage.

All realized wealth is transfigured Force; and want of it, a sure sign of sterility and degeneracy. Industrialism is the manipulation of Force—by Force. Brains and muscles are part of the mechanism of gravitation. Descendents of "prisoners-of-war" have been trained for ages in servitude: and they make most intelligent mechanics, specialists, and serving-men.

Capital is concentrated Force, applied to the extraction and storage of additional Force. It may be operated by its proprietor in any way that he pleases. He is under no obligation to others as to its application or proprietorship. He can 'do as he likes with his own' *as long as he has the Power.* He may own the earth by its agency, if he wants to; and he may buy or sell men and nations, if he feels so inclined or thinks is profitable. There is in Nature no limit to his energies or ambitions. All that is needed is Power equal to the design. But the same principles may be acted upon by any other man or association of men; and in the conflict that ensues, *Fitness is proved—absolutely and without doubt.* The 'rights of the rich' are what they *can* maintain; and the 'rights of the poor' are no less. No bounds are set to the accumulation of property, and none whatever to its re-distribution. Fair-play is not even an essential or a requisite. It may be established, if mutually desired by both combatants; but it may be wholly dispensed with. In real life it *is* always "dispensed with" by those who possess a preponderance of material might.

Equality can only exist amongst equals. Civilization implies division of labor and division of labor implies subordination and subordination implies injustice and inequality. Woe to me if I speak not truth!

At such words as these, pusillanimity blanches with timidity—gathers in its Idol Halls, supplicating—"Lord have mercy upon us!—Christ have mercy upon us!—Deliver us from Evil!"

In primitive communities the Philosophy of Power is thoroughly understood and acted upon by all classes—even by the Servi.* The ideas of abstract justice, righteousness, non-resistance, can find no lodgement in an uncorrupted brain. Life is too grim in a camp of hunters and of warriors, for artificialism to meet with anything more appreciative than a good natured sarcasm. He who has to hunt for his family-dinner every forenoon (and seize land on which to build his shelter) is not over likely to enthusiastically swallow the depraved theoria of self-renunciation, or pledge unbounded allegiance to a self-appointed Ring of tax-gatherers—masquerading as political philanthropists. He maintains his own inherent independent royalty, as long as he *can*; and never surrenders, except before absolutely superior force. Even then he vows limitless vengeance and obligates his sons and son's sons, to undying hatred against the domination and spoliation, of his conquerers.

❦10❦

In Evolution there is no finality. It is operating always in some form; endeavoring to blot out inferior organisms, and perpetuate more perfect types. Like the gods of Antiquity, it is both a Destructive and a Creative. The Powerful of the past were overthrown by the more Powerful of the present; and in strict sequence, the Powerful of to-day must be overthrown by—the more Powerful of to-morrow.

---

* Latin root-word of servant. Applied indiscriminately to mules, eunuchs, slaves, philosophers, historians, scribes, prisoners-of-war or working-cattle generally.

All 'moral' dogmatisms and religiosities, are positive hindrances to the evolution of the Higher Manhood; inasmuch as men who honestly grasp at Morals, do not as energetically grasp at Power—power being essentially non-moral. Consequently the struggle between the propertied and the propertyless classes, is not as keen as Nature evidently intends it to be. The moral man is a feeble antagonist to non-moral generalship. He foolishly permits talkative personalities (with sharper perceptive qualities), to wield unlimited Authority over him, under numerous plausible pretexts, and deliberately plunder him of his Property.

There is far and away too much weepful *mea culpa* about the average mannikin. Hence the woes of the world!—Hence the origin of the morbid craving by Dwindlings for what they call "a peaceful solution of the social problem." Weak natures are terrorized at the idea of what "might happen" in a death grapple with entrenched adversaries equally as strong, if not stronger than themselves. That is the true reason why rich men are so anxious at all times to avoid discussion, and 'maintain the Peace' and why poor men—"hunger with fatness around them, and thirst while the waters flow near: for the Law and the Gospel hath damned them, and dulled all their senses with fear."

The fact is that both sides are afraid of each other—afraid of the only rational solution.

My curse be upon the white-livered and the meek: the shameful dwindlings—who call themselves the "virtuous" the "law-abiding" the "righteous" the "godly"; the "obedient-ones!" May civilization pump its vile narcotism through the flacid ventricles of their pigeon-hearts! May they inhale brain-leprosy through the open windows of their Temples-of-Soot; and may their noisome swineries and splendid Ergastuli, be unto them living tombs! May they 'earn' their bread (also that of their conquerors) by the slimy sweat of dishonored brows; and may they perish at last like abandoned curs! May they vegetate in poverty and die in contempt. May the evil works of their 'genius' be ploughed under with Babylon and Ninevah, Anahuac and Rome! May the annals of their dismal dominion become, as the folk-tale of a fearsome nightmare that once rolled over the brain of Mankind—finally dissipating itself 'midst thunders and lightnings and the breaking up of the great deep! Verily! Verily! let them have their Reward!

It is customary for atrophied minds (like Bluntschili) to urge that the promulgation of such grim thoughts 'endanger the foundation of Society.' Even supposing that to be so, what is Society anyhow, that its "foundations" should not be threatened? Is "Society" something immaculate, something divine, something anointedly ultra-human—something that must be safeguarded, right or wrong? Is it another sacred Mount Moriah Temple—a Urim and Thummim—an Ark of the Covenant—a Sanctum Sanctorum, or merely "an ass's head hidden behind a veil?" Why should the phrase "Society in danger" be equivalent to the proclamation of a rigid taboo or a fanatical crusade? Why?

Society is altogether a matter of convenience—an implement— an expediary. It is the creation of man and what man manufactures he may modify or destroy.

Society may be defined as an agglomeration of carnivorous and herbivorous animals, seeking their natural prey and browsing along on whatever nutriment they pick-up. It is nothing more than a 'herd' of two-legged cattle and there's nothing supernatural or divine about a herd. Indeed the word herd always suggests Gadara. Human swarms have been integrated and disintegrated ten thousand times ten thousand by the centrifugal and centripetal energy of individuals.

Societies have risen and Societies have fallen; but man, the Unit—the germ-plasm—persists, with the rising of the sun, and the fall of the tides. Man is not only the 'clay,' but also the 'potter'— the paramount determinant. His fate is in his own hands absolutely, within the length of his tether.

"To the Strong all laws are cobwebs" (Solon) and when Society becomes irksome to the Strong they may dissolve it; nay it is their positive duty to dissolve it; otherwise it becomes their master and consequently their enemy and oppressor. "Society in danger" therefore is merely the hysteria of the megalomaniac.

Society (in some shape) must exist, as long as there are two human beings left alive: for companionship is as natural to the homo, as swarming is to the bee. When however the word "Society" develops into a synonym for socialistic restraint, then it becomes a menace to the Evolution of the Type and ought to be broken up accordingly—without overmuch ceremony. Friendship is necessary and ennobling, but impersonal despotism is destructive of all dignity and manly virtue.

The real danger is, that innocent and natural combinations for mutual pleasure, comradeship, profit, and defense, may transform themselves gradually into organized majority-box tyrannies— enslaving institutionalisms of the most dictatorial and obnoxious character. When Society is thus transfigured into a vast blackmailing corporation the lives and property of its component units are absolutely at its mercy, and it therefore ought to be disintegrated, consciously, deliberately, pitilessly, and at whatever cost. Freedom cannot be bought too dear for life without liberty is pandemonium.

119

Government and Society are two distinct entities, and care must be taken not to confound them. Society is the growth of mutual tolerance, friendship, and obligation; but 'government' arises from physical force applied by the Strong to the control and exploitation of vanquished foes. The sanction of government, is the same that holds good throughout the whole zoological and heliocentric scale—the sanction of material might. That 'sanction' should always be under test; because the most abject weakling may brandish a sword, but we do not know he is a weakling until another sword in the grip of a Man is pointed at his throat.

Beowulf, a Saxon song-master, apostrophising "the Sword," voices this primeval Organon as it was instinctively understood by our ancestors.

"The war-thing! the comrade! father of honor, and giver of kingship! the fame-smith!—the songmaster! Clear singing! clean slicing! sweet spoken! soft finishing! making death beautiful—life but a coin—to be staked in the pastime; whose playing is more than transfer of being. Arch-anarch! chief builder! prince and evangelist! I am the will of God! I am the Sword!"

It is only in ages saturated in atmospheres of brain-wrecking artificialism—in consumptive communities steeped to the very lips in elemental error—that senile, degrading, anthropomorphic myths and manias are substituted for hard, bitter Common-Sense. (All great truths are "hard" and "bitter," but Lies, to the morbidly inclined, are sweeter than wild honey.)

One by one we abandon Realisms—to follow *fata morganas.* We are mortgaging our destiny to the Pawnbrokers of Decadence. Behold!—the legerdemain of the Orient demonetizes the Manhood of the West!

We fight like women, and feel as much,
The thoughts of our heart we guard—
Where scarcely the scorn of a god could touch,
The sneer of a fool hits hard,
The treacherous tongue and the cowardly pen,
The weapons of curs decide—
They faced each other and fought like men;
In the days when the world was wide.*

And yet the world is beautiful—as beautiful as a blushing maiden dreaming of her first lover. "Fair laughs the morn and soft the breezes blow" and *men* only await *Captaining* to—capture and possess.

---

* Henry Lawson, Angus & Robertson, Melbourne, Australia.

120

MANHOOD IS DEMONETIZED

This little pamphlet has been issued, not for private profit, but to assist in uprooting the alien and pernicious Ideals that have been for long centuries corrupting the blood and corroding the brain of Europe and America. Conventional moral dogmas and political standards-of-value are, like wooden idols, the work of men's hands. They have no real basis in Nature nor have they any supernatural sanction. Every one of them has been carved out of a wormeaten lie, a brazen assumption or a madman's dream. They are impositions most insolent. Why should we bow down even in formal adulation before imbecile and unnatural principles invented thousands of years ago for the enslavement of oriental decadents! Have we not given lip-service long enough to false heroisms, and fool evangels? Why feign the possession of slave virtues?

Why continue to glorify untruths that we know to be untruths? Why should men of sterling worth obey any other man's 'thou shalt'? Let us return to Nature for our moral standards!

Let us search our own hearts and brains for the true meaning of Right and Wrong.

We are living and dying (mostly dying) in a poisonous environment of deep seated moral dementia, social disease and political illusions.

The 'Righteous and Just'! hypocrites! deceivers! Enemies of all that is noble, courageous and manly!

Destroyers of self-assertiveness! Annihilators of heroism! Would that I had a legion of demons to wring thy neck!

A crucified Jew slave (terrorized under Authority) is set up as a god, as a standard of measurement for all mankind. That is why personal valor and nobility of thought are at such a tremendous discount.

Christiandom is in bondage! Manhood is demonetized! Our race is betrayed!

121

⚡6⚡

LOVE AND WOMEN AND WAR

The best fighters are the best race-producers. This is the verdict of Biology and the instinctive belief of the whole Feminine world in general.

In the molding of Organic Nature into all its diverse forms, Love and War (with their attendant penalties and correlated consequences) are the two most potent factors. Battle is the furnace-alembic that has been consciously provided for chemically separating the animate Refuse from the Gold. Sexual desire is the amalgam that thereafter unites the golden particles, perpetuating for ages and ages the selected qualities—of physical beauty, vigor, bravery, endurance—or vice-versa. "I am convinced," writes Darwin, "that natural selection has been the main, but not the exclusive means of modification."

The same thought has been gemmed in a more sentimental but equally suggestive setting, by Dryden:

Happy, happy, happy pair,
    None but the brave,
    None but the brave,
None but the brave deserve the fair.

Heraclitus condensed it into the terser dictum 'strife is the *parent* of things.' Even Solomon (the hoary old kingling) chanted it in characteristic Oriental strophes: "Love is stronger than death, the coals thereof are coals of fire, which hath a most vehement flame. Many waters cannot quench love, neither can the flood drown it—*Jealousy is as cruel as the grave.*"

Fighting is the method whereby the most fitted to propogate conclusively prove the fact. Animals, plants, birds, reptiles, and fish, all exist in surroundings of unending sex-rivalry and warfare—so do men. Organic life is one ceaseless round of Love and War. Sexualism and slaughter go hand in hand.

Bacteria butchers bacteria—germ wars with germ—shark eats the shark—tigers struggle with tigers—the lion rends lion—eagle kills eagle, and man fights man, for the favor of the female—or the plunder of the vanquished. "Peace on earth and mercy mild," is mere lunacy-babblement. Even sheep, the most "Christly" of animals, wage tremendous duels—in due season.

There is no other earthly passion so fiercely, savagely egotistic, as sexual desire and it is the physical basis of all human "love"—even the most ethereal and romantic. Everywhere 'the season of love, is the season of battle,' and when the fires of sexualism burn low in nations or men, they are as unfit for freedom, as they are unfit to reproduce their kind.

Topinard explains how sexualism operates among Vertebrates of the deep: "The male Artocephali (sea-bear) arrive at the Falkland Islands in November, and scatter out along the beach. In December the females arrive, and immediately violent battles are being fought in all directions for their possession. Family life follows exactly as among humans. If the females behave badly, the male chastises them: they crouch at his feet, seem to beg his pardon, and shed copious tears. At times the male and female weep together."

A geographer and naturalist of world-repute (A.R. Wallace) proclaims a series of similar facts—facts that are not new to observant minds:

"Among the higher animals it is a very general fact, that the males fight together for the possession of the females. This leads...to the stronger or better armed males, becoming the parents of the next generation, which inherits the peculiarities of the parents; and thus vigor and offensive weapons are continually increased in the males, resulting in the strength and horns of the bull, the tusks and shield of the boar, the antlers and fleetness of the stag, and the spurs and fighting instincts of the gamecock. But almost all male animals fight together, though not specially armed; even hares, moles, squirrels, and beavers, fight to the death. The same rule applies to all male birds. From this very general phenomenon, there necessarily results a form of natural selection, *which increases the vigor and fighting power of the male animal; the weaker being either killed, wounded, or—driven away.*"—as among men.

In his *Descent of Man*, Darwin makes a similar general statement: "With social animals, the young males have to pass through many a contest, before they win a female, and the older males have to retain their females by renewed battles. They have also, as in the case of mankind, to defend their females, as well as their young, *from enemies of all kinds*, and to hunt for their joint subsistence."

123

Among the Vertebrates, the king of the herd (or pack), selects himself by his battle-prowess—upon the same "general principles" that induced Napoleon to place the Iron Crown upon his own brow—*with his own hand.* All the Regal Houses of the world have been founded by fighting-men, and upheld by—fighting-men; just as in the "brute" creation. The chief recommendation to both animal and human Chieftainship, is fighting capacity. The "common herd" instinctively feels that a *good* fighter possesses all the requisite virtues of *good* leadership, and leadership is exactly what they want. By conquest alone can an animal-king be deposed, and his vanquisher is *always* his successor. As long as his sight, hearing, strength, and courage endures, he is absolute lord, judge, procreator-in-chief—*but not one moment longer.* 'The king's dead, long live the king' is a biological affirmative.

This is the Natural Order. The un-natural order is to appoint feeble but eloquent rhetoricians as Chief Magistrates (or constitutional kinglings). This latter plan is adopted only by human swarms in eras of senility and wholesale decadence.

Politicians are everlastingly "fighting" each other (if we believe the sensational headlines of our editorial *Daily Liar*) but that kind of warfare is a sham intended to deceive. No real "fight" ever takes place between them. What they call 'fighting' is gambling with "Ayes" and "Nays"; playing pitch-and-toss for the booty other men win and the harvests other men garner. Hark! do you hear them frothing at the mouth, loudly professing their "divine enthusiasm for Humanity." For what? In order that they (squalid scoundrels that they are) may sit on the seats of the mighty and steer the nation down to hell while putting money in their purses with taxes and blackmail. Nations have always risen to their highest pitch of fame and prosperity under the guidance of mighty men of valor, self elected: and they've sunken to the lowest depths of degradation and dishonor under the diabolical domination of elective rhetoricians. (Their ravages are not so obtrusive in America as in Europe, because territory here has been so vast—practically limitless.)

 2

Women instinctively admire soldiers, athletes, kings, nobles, and fighting-men generally, above all other kinds of suitors—and rightly so.

Nothing so lowers a lover in a virile maiden's estimation, than for him to be "whipped" in a personal encounter with a rival.

Among all classes of females this sentiment persists. The best bid a man can make for the admiration of any woman (even the most pious) is a display of undaunted physical prowess.

Young women have an instinctive detestation for the "good young man that dies" kind of adorer, and they positively abhor the pale coward—even though he be a blood relation. Strength, energy-of-character, ferocity, and courage, she admires in her possible husband, above all other qualities combined. Even to be carried-off by force, is not repugnant to her feelings, if the "bold bad man" is in other respects acceptable.

She pines to be 'wooed and *won*' (or as it were) she likes to feel that she has been mastered, conquered, taken possession of—that the man who has stormed her heart is in all respects, a *man* among men. This suggestive female idiosyncracy is rhythmically set forth by an anonymous writer thus: "Down a winding pathway in a garden old, tripped a beautous maiden, but her heart was cold. Came a prince to woo her, *said* he loved her true; maiden said he didn't, so he ceased to woo. Came a perfumed noble—dropping on one knee; *said* his love was deeper, than the deepest sea. But the winsome maiden, said his love was dead, and the perfumed noble, accepted what she said. Came a dashing Stranger, took her off by force: said he'd *make* her love him, and she did—of course."

Conquersome personalities by obtaining possession of the best and handsomest females raise up as a rule, conquersome descendents. Hence the origin of Great Races. Second-class males are driven by necessity to mate with second-class females; and in strict sequence third-class males select partners from feminine remainders. (Hence the stereotyped nature of servile Castes.)

Superior males *take* racially superior women, and inferior males are permitted to duplicate themselves, per media of inferior feminines. Each class reproduces its kind (on the average) and if the ordained struggle for earth's Good-Things is not artificially interfered with, the leading classes are periodically called upon to maintain their pre-eminence at every turn, by Might or be swept away, enslaved, supplanted, expropriated by the braver and bolder Animals.

Aristocracies have always originated in War. Sham ones grow up (like mushrooms) in times of peace. No "Aristocracy" ought to be allowed to dominate one moment longer, than it is able to maintain itself, by the edge of the Sword. Again, subordinated classes should not permit themselves to be mastered by Usurpers who cannot fight. It is the Natural Order for first-class men to dominate third-class men—but the classes are self-selective; by conflict. Someday inferior breeds will be remorselessly exterminated, as useless and noxious vermin. Behold! I judge the future by the evolutionism of the Past.

Women congregate at athletic sports and gladiatorial contests; impelled by the same universal instinct that induces the lioness to stand expectantly by, while two or more rival males are ripping each other to pieces in a rough-and-tumble—for her possession. The lioness submits, as a matter of choice, to the embraces of the Victor; and in the most fashionable society, the stalwart footballer or the dashing soldier, has practically unlimited selective powers, among the marriageable maidens of his own particular set.

No nation, no empire, has ever fallen—no race has ever been enslaved, *because* it delighted in manly sports—in the hunting of boars and lions, and men—in deadly tournaments—in deuling— in prize fighhting—in gladiatorial combats—in scenes of "cruelty and blood." No! not one! (Nature is cruel—a million times more cruel than man ever was.) But dozens of 'civilizations' have perished shamefully, ignominiously, *because* of the spreading canker of personal cowardice—gendered by effeminacy, luxury, usury, laboriousness, statecraft, superstition, 'culture,' and peace.

Want of daring—enfeeblement of physique—meanness of mind—fear of danger and dread of death (sure signs of racial deterioration) have *never originated* with athletic tournaments, nor wars of conquest, nor gladiatorial games. When Clericalism abolished the 'holmgang' the pride of Norland silently waned away: when it abolished the Olympian games Greece rotted with decay; and when it banned gladiatorial contests the Eternal City "had its day."

Bull-dog virtues are bound to triumph in the long run and they can only be developed (if developed at all) by daily practice from youth up. Hence the necessity of 'brutal' football—'brutal' warfare—'brutal' personal encounters—'brutal' thoughts and 'brutal' combinations. (The word 'brutal' is written here because it is popularly misunderstood and used as a missile.) The 'brutal' races have always been supremely 'brutal.' (Alexander, Sesostric, Ceaser, Titus, Nero, Bonaparte, Cromwell, Grant, Bismarck, Cecil Rhodes.)

The word 'brutal' in real life means the reverse of effeminate. A man is brutal who will not turn the other cheek. *What is it "brutes" do that in nature, is wrong?*

Emerson perceived this pivotal anachronism clearly when he declared: 'Nature is erect, but man is fallen.' Christlings are forever using the word 'brutal' to terrorize each other but who are they anyhow? Are they not the scum, and dross, and offscourings, and creeping things, of the Aryan migrations—mere shrieking, blubbering, fulminating dwindlings of the very lowest intellectual development? Let Emerson again be put on the witness stand. He may be considered fairly impartial. Hear what he has to say:

The waves unashamed, in difference sweet,
Play glad with the breezes; old play-fellows meet.
The journeying atoms primordial wholes,
Firmly drawn, firmly driven by their animate poles,
Sea, earth, air, silence; plant, quadruped, bird;
By one music enchanted; one deity (nature) stirred.
Each the other adorning, accompanying still;
Night veileth the morning; the vapor, the hill.
Man crouches and blushes, absconds and conceals,
He creapeth and sneaketh, he palters and steals.
Infirm, melancholy, jealous;—glancing around;
An oaf, an accomplice; he poisons the ground.

Athletic contests (and combats of all kinds), have a powerful influence in molding for the better, the personnel of all participants therein. He who *must* meet worthy antagonists face-to-face and deafeat them or be himself defeated, ennobles his own mentality—unconsciously. Courage, coolness, intrepidity, purity of blood, and mental balance, are the athlete's first requisites. He must therefore be individualistic, self-reliant and calmly resourceful; i.e., he *must* be brave.

The brave man is ever generous, frank, outspoken, dauntless. His brow is open—his step fearless and firm—his bearing self-poised, leonine. He looks at you without a tremor—sums you up at a glance, and in business affairs, his "word of honor" is more binding than Shylock's sealed bond. He may not be an erudite philosopher—a profound scholar—nor an eminent elocutionist— (nor be troubled over much with the "saving" of his soul) but he is more than all that—*he is a man.* Hence, everywhere he is first favorite, especially with the feminine gender—whose sexual instincts are as true to Nature as the needle is to the pole.

What a tremendous difference is noticeable, between the self-contained bearing of the bronzed soldier; and the creeping sauvity of the chalky-skinned shopkeeper—the vileness of the Hebrew money-lender—the sweet milk-and-honeyness of the venemous pastor—the base obsequiousness of the lean hireling—the boorishness of the ungainly peasant—and the fat sleek cunning of the tax-eating political? Who can look upon them (bunched together) and honestly affirm, that—fighting does not tend to improve the stamina, beauty, vigor, and seed of the race?

Healthy animalism is the foundation of all virtues whatsoever. Diseased bodies produce diseased minds. Hence the noxious degeneracy of the average 'genius.' Hence also the shrieking madness of the blinded multitude. Average 'civilized' men are more or less abortions anyhow—pre-natal megalomaniacs. Sane men could never be induced to worship an Idol (made out of a mendicant Jew) nor would they consciously erect in the name of Progress, State sausage mills for chewing up their own flesh, and sucking their children's marrow bones. (Deranged minds while being very susceptible to suggestion, possess—no initiative.)

It is the gibbering "geniuses" that are luring mankind down to eternal damnation. If these monstrous mattoids had been smothered the day they were born—the earth and the air would have been purer, to that extent. Have they not innoculated the human race with every malady; while proclaiming nostrums and "infallible remedies"—for each incurable disease?

From pulpit, platform and library, they ray out their maniacal babblement; and rabbles, madder than march-hares, suck it all in, with open-mouthed wonderment!

Hark! do you hear consumptive fiendlings coughing out their literary pestilence in the High Places of the World? They would cure "the sufferings of the submerged," would they?

Vain is the medicament that expels no contagion! Vain also is the rhetoric that cures no human woe!

 3

Women take supreme delight in the roll of warlike drums—in the marching of the military, in reading the poems and romances of 'battle, murder and sudden death.' (Police Gazettes are mostly supported by women, because of the sensational homicidal reports.)

French women (even against their deep patriotic sentimentalism) admired the fine physique and martial bearing of the German troops that poured through Paris in '71. The contrast between the tall, clean-skinned German Conquerers and the dwarfishness of the French National Guards was then most strikingly displayed. Clericalism there has had full sway for centuries and now majority-box socialism (also cynical squalid sensualism) is all the rage.

Whenever soldiers conquer in war, they also conquer in love—after the first paroxysm of revengeful patriotism is over. Women of vanquished races are usually very prone to wed with the men who have slaughtered their kindred in battle.

Rudyard Kipling, in one of his popular ballads touches upon this ethic peculiarity with a masterly hand: "By the old Moulmein Pagoda looking eastward to the sea, there's a Burmah girl a settin', an I know she thinks o' me; for the wind is in the palmtrees, and the temple bells, they say: 'Come you back O British Soldier, come you back to Mandalay.'"

After the battle of Senlac, Norman adventurers were the 'prey' of fair-haired Saxon maidens. To this hour, wherever soldiers or men-o-wars-men go, amorous dusky daughters of conquered Islands, absolutely leap into their arms. New Zealand Maori women married British officers, soldiers and sailors in thousands and when the regiments were sent home many men remained rather than break up their families. At Gibralter, Spanish senoritas literally storm that rock-ribbed fortress to get at the "widows'-sons." The loves of Red Indian maidens for Pale Face warriors may some day find a Homer, to clothe them with immortality. Already many have become world-famous; notably the epic Pocohontas and that erratic filibuster John Smith. Since the marriage of Strongbow to Eva the admixture of Celt and Sassanach blood has proceeded continuously from the same root cause. In garrison towns it is a matter of perpetual witticism the preference which females of all satraps display for soldier lovers.

What modern Gaul requires to reinvigorate her ethnic stamina is wholsesale and limitless conquest by some Northern Race. The conquerers, by seizing all the land and movable property, would become immediately a ruling caste, attracting to themselves all the best feminines of France. This infusion of new blood would *not* strengthen the inherited physique of the invaders but it would certainly invigorate the structural physique of the defeated tribe.

No hand should be stretched forth to shield a self-poisoned breed of humans from utter subordination, for an undue preponderance of weakly organisms is not desireable. It is good that they should be swept away and it is better that they should be swept away by war than by pestilence—as in China and India. Enslavement or annihilation is the just reward of wholesale physical debilitation. The Blackfeet's ruthless warfare against the Digger Indians was in strict accord with the Cosmic Plan.

The story of the past literally bristles with illustrations of ethnic displacement, carried out (unconsciously perhaps) as herein set forth. But to resume the personal factor. Briseis, after her "dearly beloved" had been slain by Achilles, consoled herself with the self-delightful fact that the slayer would take her, as spoil, to his own bed. The Valkyries (Norse battle-maidens) married *only* with their conquerors. After the storming of Troy, there was very little ceremony over the union of Ajax and Cassandra, in the temple of Minerva. All through the Illiad epic, women are at once the property, the conquerer's prize, and the inspiration of all the Homeric Warriors.

It is notorious that when Roman and Greek matrons discovered no parental virility in their debauched consorts, they deliberately made advances to the blonde-bearded barbarians, who had been imported from the frontiers (prisoners of war) to wrestle in the amphitheatre. Many a dark-eyed patrician 'maiden of Italia' throbbed with secret joy, at the duel-victory of her favorite fighter; and many another has wept her eyes out, as the greedy remorseless sand, drank up the heart's blood of her "dying gladiator." American women's passion for marrying foreigners, arises more or less, from similar instincts. American born men evince an alarming tendency toward impotency. (Vide census returns.) An immense number of them are 'old before they are young' and a very large proportion (more especially in the cities) are lean lantern jawed profligates, or leering bald-headed wrecks.

The noblest born maids and matrons of Rome vied with each other for Ceasar's smile—when (after killing one million men, and enslaving two million) he became Imperator. Queens were proud to be his concubines; and one of his own natural sons (without knowing the fact) helped to assassinate him. The love scandals of David, Solomon, Aaron Burr, Sigurd the Volsung, Hercules, Jupiter, Apollo, Jehovah, Isis, Sir Galahad, Charles II, Henry VIII, Bonaparte, Alexander, Raleigh, and that dashing triumvir Marc Antony, have affected, for better or for worse, the whole world.

'Better the mistress of a king, than the wife of a subject,' was a saying once popular amongst European women, in the ages when kings were really kings of men—when they were mail-clad sword-swingers—mighty men-of-valor. Modern "kings" are simulacra—dilettantes, scarecrows—robed in purple, and paid liberal salaries to impersonate regalism for the delectation of the vulgar. Marionettes are they!—fitted only to lay foundation-stones—utter vicarious homilies—read off type-written deceptions; or now and then dress up in swashbuckler accoutrements, to review Messrs Rothschild, Ikelheimer, Bleichroder & Co's praetorian guards, marching by in serried column—with nodding plumes and bannered panoply of war.

Modern kings are degenerates; even more so (if that be possible) than their laborious subjects. They have allowed all kingly Initiative to be wrested from them, by the diabolical cunning of that 'plastic demon' the Jew Banker—that Mephistophelian manipulator of National Debts and National Credits. Kings have not been equal to the occasion and resultantly they and their brain-drugged subjects are "bonded" to the Israelite. The Jew has been supinely permitted to do—what Alexander, Ceasar, Nusherwan, and Napoleon failed to accomplish—crown himself Emperor of the World; and collect his vast tributes from 'the ends of the earth.' From the Mississippi valley to the plains of the Hoang-Ho—from Spitzbergen's icy uplands to New Zealand's iron shores—his satraps bear sway, and his tax-gatherers pillage, ravage, and rob. As long as the Aryan Race bows down (even nominally) at the Sign of the Cross, or vacuously endeavors to 'keep the commandments,' it is hopelessly entangled—it is delivered up—a burnt sacrificial offering—to the dolabra of the sons of Jacob—Jacob the supplanter.

Maimonides the philosopher of Hebraism boldly suggested this view to orthodox Talmudists: "The teachings of the Christian Church," he proclaimed, "tend to bring to perfection all mankind, so that they *serve* Jehovah with one consent. For, since the whole world is thus full of the words of the Messiah; of the teachings of the Holy Writ, and the Commandments, these words have spread to the ends of the earth, even if any man deny the binding character of them now." Which being interpreted meaneth: Tolerate O children of Israel, the false religion of the Crucified Prophet! It will serve your ends most admirably. When the tribes of the West 'serve Jehovah with one consent'—Behold! they shall also serve you. Christ shall 'bring them to perfection,' and ye shall put them in bonds. They have made you weep and suffer; ye shall make them drip tears of blood; for the Lord your God hath said it.

Nineteen centuries of evangelation (with a Hebrew bible as basis) has resulted in—what? The political, social, financial, and philosophical domination of—the Hebrew. We study his falsified chronicles, his melancholy literature, and his prophetic outpourings, as if alone, in such a nauseous heap of rubbish and stench the *summum bonum* was to be found. Not an acre changeth hands—not a battle-ship lifts an anchor—not a ploughshare cleaves the soil—not a president vetos a Bill—not a diplomat signs a protocol—not an emperor waves a saber, without direct inspiration from the hidden Hebrew Potentate. Behold!— "the King is in his counting-house, counting out his money"— and such a king! Israel is absolute dictator, because he is absolute Proprietor. The gold *and the silver* and the credits of the world belong to him, and as long as he hires politicians to utlize the military arm of 'government,' in the collection of his 'loans'—in defense of his ironclad safety-vaults, he is an irresponsible Jehovah-Jirah. But should Force ever fail him, "the lean dogs outside the wall" will leap snarling upon him and spoil him of his spoil; that the fittest may survive.

"The Jews are ministers of Gold—Great Bankers who see in the People and the State a mine to be worked."* "Our life blood is

---

* M. Anatole L. Beaulieu, *Revue des Deux Mondes*, 1896.

drawn from us by these harpies of finance and the gaming table, who mock us with illusions, while they strip us of our all."** "The harm which the Jews commit does not come from individuals, but from the very constitution of these people; they are locusts, caterpillars, which ravage France, to whom commerce ought to be prohibited."***

There are two distinct yet parallel species of the parasitical Semite: the first, represented by Marx, Lasalle, Stepniak, and Jesus-the-dreamer: the second, by Goshen, Rothschild, Baring, and Iscariot-the-Banker. Between them they've practically extinguished civil liberty and personal independence, wherever they have been sheltered. Viper like, do they not bite the very mamae that gives them suck? What have they ever done to Gaul but eat her heart out; and Gaul was first to "emancipate" them? What are they now doing to Germany, Russia, England, America, Africa, Australia? Poisoning the brain-cells of the enslaved multitude while taking-in-pledge—the plough and the harrow—the millstones and the mill.

Over nations and empires and colonies in vassalage, hangs the Idol-sign of the Brazen Crucifix (that sures no ill). Over a world in bondage looms the dread shadow of the Three Golden Balls.

 4

As the stars and the suns and primordial atoms, attract each other by odic force, so do handsome women and brave men. The nerve cells of splendid feminines and resolute warriors vibrate in rhythmic unison. Between them there is a mutual free-masonry, that neither "creed" nor "culture" has ever been able to eradicate; because it is part of the cosmic plan for evolving a higher, and yet a higher type.

Womenkind mobilize in battalions-of-beauty, at football matches, ball tournaments, acquatic carnivals, and sham battles; just as the feminines of "Auld-lang-syne" gathered at the archery sports—the Colosseum combats—the Olympian games, and the Neolithic war-dances. In their worship of the warrior, Indian squaws, lionesses and ball-room belles are in harmonious accord.

Even in years of peace (peace may be considered a temporary truce—a partial suspension of the struggle for survival) civilians in female society are at a heavy discount, when the gold-braided naval lieutenant or the 'Captain-in-his-whiskers' is prowling around. At balls and receptions, the martial uniform carries all

** Wilson, Financial Editor, *Investor's Review*, London.
*** Emporer Napoleon the First—Quoted by *Presence*.

132

before its sexuality (more especially if there be a *man* inside) just as it does among the head hunters of Borneo, the cannibals of the Congo, the redskins of Oklahoma—or the gruesome savages of Chicago.

University professors (priests disguised) and supersanct demagogues, may rail in florid prose and honeyed lines or rhyme, against 'militarism' and the 'horrors of war,' but they might, much more logically, rear-up on their hind legs and bray furiously at the belts of Orion; or kick out in silly desperation, at the glancing spears of the Northern Lights.

Those literary 'luminaries' (whose business is to dwarf public opinion) with spectacles on their noses—madness in their cerebrums—congestion in their livers—saplessness in their bones—fear in their hearts and pens between their snaky fingers, are never enthusiastically "selected" by virile women. When these poor miserable manlings (geniuses they name each other) do happen (by some lucky chance), to get a woman, they make her life a torment, and scarcely ever leave any progeny behind them, for the doom of degeneracy is upon every nerve and filament of their bodies. Who ever heard of a lovelorn virgin risking her life, or her reputation, to mate herself with a sanctimonious creeping-thing, or bespectacled savant? Did you ever look upon a great drama wherein the hero did not do a bit of fighting? Prince Charming is ever a performer of gallant actions—he conquers giants—outwits knaves—slaughters monsters—pulverizes wicked enchanters and is an all around perambulating Terror to the wicked—that is to say to "the other fellow."

A recent account of the Indian mutiny, states that the first outbreak (at Meerut) was precipitated by 'a splendid native girl, hung with jasmine garlands' who womanlike, taunted her sepoy lover by hissing in his face, when he came to visit her: "We of the bazaar kiss no cowards." He left her in a rage and went out to recklessly precipitate Insurrection, that ended by the blowing of "the defeated" from the mouths of the conqueror's cannon.

As agents provocateurs, women have never been surpassed by men. Cornelia trained up her two brilliant sons, with a view to hurl them against and overturn the Roman Oligarchs; a city harlot led the *Sans-Cullotes* of the French Revolution. Queen Boadicea led her own army of painted Britons against the, then all-conquering, Legions of Rome. A female epileptoid (since canonized) dressed herself in iron armor, mounted a war-horse, and urged her demoralized countrymen—to the forcible expulsion of an alien army. In American wars the feminine has also played her part with eclat; and she delights (above all other women) in tracing her own and her family's pedigree to Revolutionary

133

Soldiers, Pirates, Filibusters; and through them to the mail-clad knights and heros of long ago. No Public Library in this Republic is without its complete set of Stud-Books, and none are deeper students thereof than—women. Instinctively comprehending the determinant power of heredity, these students are vaguely endeavoring (in their own peculiar way), to solve the renowned Spencerian Synthetic: "Having seen that matter is indestructible, motion continues, and Force persistant—having seen that Forces are everywhere undergoing transformation; that motion always follows the line of least resistance; is invariably rhythmic; it remains to discover the similarly invariable formula, expressing the combined consequences of the actions, thus separately formulated."

Herod's wife and daughter, and their secret alliance for getting John the Baptizer's head chopped off, must not be overlooked; nor the calculated 'brutality' with which Jael drove that tent-peg into General Sisera's cranium, when he slept. The folk-tale of Delilah and Samson is also to the point. In many respects women have proved themselves more cruel, avaricious, blood-thirsty and revengeful than men.

Women are also remarkably good liars. Deception is an essential and necessary part of their mental equipment. They are inherently deceitful. Men however reckon upon that and discount it well in advance. Without deception of some sort, a woman would have no defense whatever, against rivals, lovers, or husbands. We must not forget that women really hate each other—intensely.

It is as natural for women to prevaricate, as it is for man to resent a blow on the face. It is their weapon. Hence they take up with false religions, priestcrafts, superstitions, much more readily than men. They like to play the hypocrite, and pretend to be "O so holy," when their secret thoughts are carnal, self-centered and materialistic. When women *think*, they think falsely—when they follow their instinct, they do exactly what nature intended them to do—limited of course by the inevital 'man'—'the brute that he is."

Women are beautiful animals, delightful companions, affectionate mothers, sisters and wives, kindhearted friends; but they are—born dissimulators.

A woman is primarily a reproductive cell-organism, a womb structurally embastioned by a protective, defensive, osseous network; and surrounded with the antennae, and blood vessels, necessary for supplying nutirment to the growing ovum or embryo. Sexualism and maternity dominate the lives of all true women. To such an extent is this so, that they have little time left (or inclination) to "think" and therefore they've never been fitted out ab-initio with reasoning organs. Probably this is what

134

Mahomet alluded to, when he sententiously affirmed that "women have no soul." (Even in man, the soul is probably a fiction, but in women its absence is an absolute certainty.) Women are made sexually attractive to equilibrate their lesser masculinity. It is man—the warrior's—business to supply their wants, and select the best of them, for his own enjoyment and the propogation of *his* seed. They will not object—except in a giggling, semi-sentimental sort of way, because they comprehend their own incapacity for self-mastership, and logical business methods. They are never touched with any sense of personal responsibility; are mere babies in worldly concerns—hysterical, well supplied with tear glands, verbal mechanisms—but lovable always. Slaves and women are notoriously incompetant of self-control—of holding their own in 'business'—when not inspired and assisted by male friends. They are intended by nature to be loved and defended but not to be "equalized."

 5

When their passions are stirred, women have performed deeds of heroism (and of terror), that even a man with nerves of steel, would hesitate at. They have fought on sea and land, the bravest of the brave. They have led armies and ruled empires, and been criminals of the darkest dye. Messaline, Aggripina, Amestes, Charlotte Corday, Elizabeth of Russia, Jael, Fulvia, Theroigne de Mericourt, Jezebel—the Borgias; have all made themselves more or less infamous. "Terrible is the rage of the billows—terrorizing is the fear of poverty, but more terrorizing than all things is the hate of a woman." (Euripides) Pseudo scientists have lately investigated "The Female Offender" with anthropometric accuracy, but their methods are puerile and unsatisfactory. Their very 'first principle' is false. They begin by assuming that the "criminal type" is to be found in jails—a most superficial and unscienctific assumption. *Only criminals who fail are found there*; and by far the largest proportion of them do not fail. Naturally enough, successful criminals have not been "investigated" by Messrs Ferreri, Lombroso, Havelock, Ellis, et. al. That being so, their sagest conclusions are vitiated. Indeed it is an accepted truism among criminals and police, that 'only the fools are caught.' Many of our most eminent men in law, medicine, science, religion and statesmanship, are criminals—criminals of the most atrocious description. The difference between the man who rules in the Castle, and the other man who is chained in the castle-dungeon, is the difference between success and failure. There is a strong affinity between the criminal and the conquerer.

If Washington for example, had failed, he would (most probably) have been hunted-down, and hung as an outlaw and traitor. However, he 'won' by *Force*, and consequently became a mighty potentate. King David was a sheep-stealer and blackmailer, until he triumphed. Then he became "a man after God's own heart." William the Norman was also a criminal, and fifty percent of his invading army were exiled outlaws; but by conquest he became king of England, and his followers blossomed into nobles.

Hence the Spencerian dictum: "The sole truth that transcends experience, by underlying it, is the Persistence of Force. This being the basis of experience, must be the basis of any scientific organization of experiences. To this an ultimate analysis brings us down; and on this a rational synthesis must be built up." *(First Principles)* Criminals and statesmen are visible embodiments of the Persistence of Force! Now that being so, scientists should define, unmistakably, what they mean by "crime," before commencing to elaborately tabulate 'the criminal type.'

But whether a criminal is successful or not, he seems to have a peculiar fascination for women. He who "risks his life to advance his fortunes" may reckon beforehand upon unlimited feminine approval. If he *succeeds* and becomes a millionaire, a chancellor, a president, or a king, he has only to 'hold up his hand' to be literally 'rushed' by the handsomest feminines in the land: and even if he fails bravely, women will gather in shoals to visit him in jail, besieging him with bouquets and proposals of marriage, even at the gallows. In Michigan a law has lately been enacted, to prohibit female adorers, from sending flowers to condemned murderers, burglars, and bank wreckers. Lombroso says somewhere that "good and passionate women have a fatal propensity to love bad men;" but with characteristic want of the logical faculty, he abstains enthusiastically, from defining 'good' and 'bad.'

Belle Starre, the border bandit (who died in a fight with State troops) was the daughter of a guerrilla chief. She selected her numerous husbands from the bravest dare-devils in her band, and on the slightest sign of cowardice, they were discarded. "I do *love* a fellow who shows grit," was a common expression of hers.

A printed catalogue of the sanguinary duels, that have been fought through jealousy, would not be less than fifty miles thick. (The mythical Cain and Abel are supposed to have quarreled over some ante-deluvian young woman's charms; and she must have married Cain.) If the duels between the animals, plants, birds, fish, germs, and infusorians, for possession of the female, were also added thereto; this planet would not contain the first chapter of the first volume. Women like to be able to say that two men have fought over them. All female animals display a similar peculiarity.

Bushrangers, freebooters, rebels, pirates, have never lacked for love romances. Plays and novels by the thousand have been written upon their escapades, and are always perennially popular. From the Arabian Nights down to Marie Correli and Ouida, it is one long rhythmic lilt of 'Love and Women and War.' Women authors are specially prone to glorify their heroes, beauty-of-form, daring, hardihood, and resolution.

Jesse James and his reckless band of outlaws, also had their famous love adventures. The mother of the James boys had her arm torn off by the explosion of a detective's bomb, thrown through her bedroom window, in the darkness of the night.

The memory of "Brennan on the Moor," (and his dashing inamorata, who "handed him a blunderbuss from underneath her cloak"), is still as green as the hillsides of Innisfail. Like Mahomet, Tell, William Wallace, Ceasar, and Napoleon, this famous outlaw's popularity rested on—a suggestive economic fact:

"He never robbed a poor man,
Upon the king's highway;
But when he'd taken from the rich,
He gave unto the poor;
So bold and undaunted,
Was Brennan on the moor."

Though not cast in the American mold, Mr. Brennan was somewhat of a "practical statesman." Decidedly!

According to Inspector Schaak's very cleverly written pamphlet, each of the Chicago bomb-throwers had his own romance. An heiress supplied money for the defense of one, whom she proposed to marry: but the most daring and logical of them all (when defeated) "fell upon his sword," like unto Brutus and Cato and Saul. That is to say, he blew his head off with explosives brought to him by his lady-love. It is also noteworthy that he was the son of a Crown Prince. Heredity therefore may have had much to do with the magnitude of his concept. *In se magna ruunt.*

Another of these slave-betrayed, mob-abandoned enthusiasts was the brother of an American General, and seems to have led a wandering adventurous life; finally falling 'head-over-heals' in love with a Southern quadroon; who still zealously fans the embers of her dead husband's agitation (limited of course by police censorship). Whenever she rises to speak in this city, she is surrounded by stenographic-mouchards and by armed officers of the "Law" in picturesque uniforms.

By direct command of the People, two of those men were choked to death and two others had their necks neatly broken; amid reverberating shouts of worldwide approbation. Their 'Power' was not equal to their 'Logic,' and consequently they were snuffed-out in strict accordance with the Law of the survival-of-the-fittest. 'They who make half-revolutions dig their own graves,' is an old Cromwellian proverb, that they had evidently failed to properly consider.

Thus the vibrations of Matter and Motion are to be seen in all social phenomena; and Regal Authority is upheld by the combined strength of arm and brain, *that gave it birth.* "Man, like every other animal, must remain subject to a severe struggle." (Darwin)

Love in sexual relationship, Power in social adjustments, Polarity and Magnetism in physics, Gravitation in astronomy, and Might in ethics, are exact synonyms—correlated phrases of one primary Assertice: "the Persistence of Force." *Se nu san—so na si.* The Sultan of Turkey has been melodramatically described by W.E. Gladstone, that "Grand Old Spider," as: "the Assassin of the Century," and yet the women of the East (even those of America), would claw each other's eyes out for half a chance to enter his harem.

Dr. Jamieson, the South African freebooter, and his chief, Cecil Rhodes, though unmercifully abused and denounced as wicked criminals, are continuously being deluged with written proposals of marriage, from heiresses on both sides of the Atlantic. These two men, by Force and Diplomacy, "stole" two million acres of the finest agricultural and pastoral land in Africa: together with gold mines, silver mines, copper mines, diamond mines, also vast herds of sheep and cattle.

They carried fire and sword into the strongholds of their enemies—shot "gods" with rifle-bullets—cut the throats of priestly sorcerers in scores—shed blood of "adversaries" like water; and reduced the defeated Kaffirs to a respectful condition of "constitutional freedom." There is no cant and hypocrisy about Cecil Rhodes! None! He is a man made whole—blunt as Napoleon or Bismarck. He is (in his own sphere) of the Ceasar, Cromwell, Darwinian stock. Believing implicitly in the survival of the fittest, he is the despair of the priestling and the terror of the politician. He laughs at their parchment Laws and shrieking Editorials—he rides rough-shod over their Golden Rules—he scorns their Sermons on the Mount—he spits upon their Tabulated 'Commandments.' He *takes* what he wants, if he has the Power—not otherwise. He does not beg—he does not pray—he does not "steal." No!—he goes direct for what he wants and "annexes" it, if he can. Nor does he weep crocodile tears, over the 'enslavement' of races that Nature manifestly stamped with inferiority. In days long gone by, such men were the norms of Anglo-Saxondom. Now! Alas! Alas! they are astounding experts.

If this Republic had produced one Cecil Rhodes forty years ago, the Civil War (provoked by idiotic emotionalism) would never have been fought. (Civil wars are necessary when a country is overstocked, but these States were not overpopulated in 1862.) Instead of 'Sounding the Jubilee' for plantation 'niggers,' he would have Sounded it for his own Race; by sending Grants and Shermans, not to plunder and devastate the Shenandoah valley and the home of Washington, but to seize, conquer, and re-colonize South and Central America, from El Paso to Cape Horn.

Among our Norse and Germanic forefathers, it was considered the saddest disgrace that could befall any matron, to be the mother of a weakling, or a laggard in war. Only for the debasing influence of priestcraft *that* would be felt by modern women—of all grades. Roman matrons have died of broken hearts and even drowned themselves in shame, at the poltroonery displayed by a son. If past generations had to depend on the sweet girly-girly fragile young thing of to-day—or the lean "lady graduate" for its reproductive Ova, we would long ago have become a swarm of ring-tailed baboons. Poor things, they also feel their artificiality—feel it in their hearts; when they look upon the spindle-shanked, mutilated males (scarecrows of men) that they are expected to "love, honor, and obey."

Over intellectualism (bad enough in a man) transfigures women into freaks. The more Animal Nature a maiden possesses; the more of a true woman she is—the better wife and mother she will make. Culture and refinement are horrible substitutes, for the grand old matronly virtues—beauty, naturalness, purity, maidenly hypnotism. Intellectualism renders more sensitive. Sensitive persons are very excitable, timid, and liable to disease. Over cultivation of the brain-cells undoubtedly produces (in both sexes) physical decay and leads toward insanity.

Women's noblest occupation is not merely to read erotic novels, pound the fiddle, waltz divinely, or fry steak and onions, but to *breed men*, to raise up a race of unsubdueable fighters—fighters for their own hand. Her vilest occupation is to duplicate anemic poltroons, creeping Judases, laborious jackasses. Therefore if she desires her sons to be brave, bold and successful in the battle of life, she should see to it that her husband is not a coward or a slave: and men ought also 'ware of marrying slave-maiden women.' This point is simply set forth in the Saga of Olaf Trygwason. Earl Rognwald had a degenerate son, who returned from a Viking-cruise without bringing any plunder. This was considered a shameful disgrace by the family. Earl Rognwald remarked: "my son is not like *my* forefathers." So he fitted the young man out afresh, saying to him: "I shall be pleased if you come not again; but I have little hope that you will ever be an honor to your kinsmen, for your mother's family are all thrall born." Have moderns ever improved on that thought?

There is nothing particularly inviting about barren, dyspeptic, blue-stocking 'New Women,' in pants and spectacles; talking idiotic snuffle through their noses; with busts made of adjustable india-rubber; with narrow or padded hips, and "wheels between their legs," scorching across the curbstones like mad. When such women are 'captured' what good are they? They won't even breed; or if they do so (by accident) their puny embryos, have to be delicately nurtured into life with steam-heated incubator-mechanisms and afterwards fed and weaned on 'the bottle.' The sons of such women—bottle fed abortions—of what good are they?

It is women of this kind (unnatural monsters they are) that cause so much domestic unhappiness. They have been "educated" along false lines, filled with bookish artificialism, and thereafter when called upon to take up their maternal duty, they are organic incapables. Hence the divorce court scandals—the fruit of wholesale degeneracy—encouraged by State interference with domestic affairs.

"Our times, in sin prolific, first
The marriage bed with taint have cursed,
And family and home—
This is the fountain head of all,
The sorrows and the ills that fall—
On Romans and on Rome." (Horace)

Gradually the curse of 'Law' invades the privacy of every home. It encourages emotional feminines to defy husbands, and Deify an irresponsible Authority. In other words it deliberately promotes unfaithfulness and unlimited free-love. It undermines the husbands Control, but at what a dreadful cost? With the "equalization" of women comes wholesale panmixia—scientific concubinage, State-regulated polyandry, and the poisoning of all inter-family intercourse. When average women find in Statute Law a "deliverer" and a "champion" more powerful than their husbands and brothers, they become both unfaithful and profligate—especially if "well educated." Then it cometh to pass (as in all ages of connubial decadence) "no man knoweth his own father." Is it not the practical tendency of the times? Again, is that 'tendency' itself not the horrible result of State-Paternalism—of Majority-Box dictation—of Statecraft and Priestcraft? The

Church lives by the functional emotionalism of women. Thus the Individual wanes and the State *grows more and more*. In *natural* society, every woman's husband is to her, both priest and king. When the baleful shadow of politics and preacherisms, looms over the marriage bed, dreadful days are at hand.

Purity of blood has played (and is yet to play) a leading role in the drama of racial evolution. Races held in bondage are necessarily mongrelized, degraded, 'equalized.' Homliness is one result of bad breeding.

When a higher type allies itself by marriage with a lower, it paves the way for its own ultimate degeneracy. When Spartans and Athenians mixed themselves with imported Asiatic and Egyptian slaves, their downfall was foretold; and when "Equality" became the motto of Christian Italy, Latins, Asiatics and Negros miscegnated, evolving the modern 'Dago'—who slaves for the descendents of the men his ancestors conquered. What a fall? Modern Greeks and Italians, with their dark complexions, curly hair and sensual lips, show distinct traces of the Negro and Asiatic blood, that (with the emancipation of the Servi) was poured into their forefathers' veins. Hence their failure in the struggle for mastery. Hence their conquest by Goth, Mongol, Teuton, Turk and Slav. A friend of Winwoode Reade's, tells a tale full of meaning. As an African explorer, he once came across a native tribe (the Joloffs) remarkable for their comparative fine appearance. He asked one of them, "how is it that everyone whom I meet here is good looking, not only your men but your women?" "That is easily explained," was the reply, "it has always been our custom to pick out our worst looking ones, and sell them for slaves."

Hybridism, south of Mason and Dixon's line, smoothed the way for the Lincoln invasion of '62 and even in the Northern States (if the present olla-podrida intermixture, with inferior breeds, is not somehow put an end to) similar invasions may be confidently predicted. Our race cannot hope to maintain its predominance, if it goes on diluting its blood with Chinamen, Negroes, Japanese, or debased Europeans. Panmixia means *both death and slavery*. Throughout South and Central America, human mongrelism is rampant (a half-breed is president of Mexico). The Latin race is hopelessly effete in both the old world and the new. Nations, like horses, are bred to win.

'Can you reverse that stupid farmer's heed,
And mend the higher by the coarser breed?'
Tremendous indeed is the occult influence of sex-love upon the evolution of organic life. Love and Glory, fidelity, emulation, resolution, beauty, strength, and courage are directly inspired by

sex-passions. In ballad and legend they are ever inextricably intertwined. 'None but the brave deserve the fair '—'Faint heart never won fair lady' and 'all is fair in love and war,' are age-worn proverbs.

Nature is saturated through and through, with the chemic potency of strife and sexualism. All the world is male and female. The saint is the only hermaphrodite. Sexual desire inspires the male with nobility of bearing; and the female with instincts of motherhood, devotedness, and song. The roar of the lion as he tosses his tawny mane, by the forest water-hole—the neigh of the high-mettled stallion, as he rears at the halter, or leaps the slip-rail—the deep challenging bellow of the shaggy bull, as he tears up the grass with his stamping hoofs—the nightingale pouring piercingly into the azure vault, its magical thrill—*man* decked in his shining regimentals, marching forth to victory or death, with drum-beat and bugle-song; all bear direct testimony to the sublime, beneficient, and all pervading Mesmerism of Force.

Military renown is now, and ever has been, the virtue of the mightiest animals. Self-abnegation is the thesis of the slave. Christlingism is functional derangement of the nerve centers—a madness—a disease.

A national Redeemer has never yet been known to materialize, in the guise of a feeble mendicant—a humble petitioner; but rather in the form of a mighty man-hunter, a destroyer of tribal ravagers—a man who saith to his disciples "come on!" not "go forth!" The Emancipator is heard of at first, with secret delight, and some misgivings; but afterwards when better understood, he comes on a war-horse with steel by his side; amid the roll of saluting cannon, the throb of triumphal drums, the fierce blare of twisted bugles, and the ringing huzzas of the People *he has enriched* by the exploitation of their foes—for all-the-world loves a fighter; especially its sisters, its cousins, and its aunts. Liberators never *arrive* from circumcised Jewry, wearing halos, briar crowns, uttering shrieks of agonized despair; nor do they "ride on a colt the foul of an ass," through the streets of Zion. No! No!—that is the ideal of—dastards and dotards.

In spite of all the century-old emasculating creeds, and debasing copy-book commercialisms, the inbred popular conception of a Mighty Man is still a Sworded Warrior—a king of men—a ruthless sweeper-away of blackmailers, userers, priests and usurpers.

"Who shall be nearest noblest and dearest, named with all honor and pride evermore? He the undaunted, whose banner is planted on Power's high ramparts, and battlements hoar. Fearless of danger, to falsehood a stranger: looking not back, when there's

142

danger before. He shall be nearest, he shall be dearest; he shall be first in our hearts evermore."

A Virginian love song expresses this grand old sentiment in its sexual form: "Rather would I view thee dying, on the last red-field of strife; 'mid thy country's heroes dying, than become—a dastard's wife."

John Ruskin (in an oft quoted passage) decidedly caught a passing glimpse of the surging logic that lurks in armed conflicts: "War is the foundation of *all* the high virtues and faculties of men. It is very strange for me to discover this, but I saw it to be quite an undeniable fact. The common notion that peace and the virtues of civil life flourished together, I found to be wholly untenable. Peace and the vices of civil-life flourish together." Decadence and Peace are concentric.

🎔 7 🎔

Next to the belted sword-swinger and the sturdy well-to-do athlete, the successful money-making 'man of affairs' is especially attractive to the average female mind. He also (in a lesser degree) is a resolute professional fighter—a scalp-hunter—his scalps being title-deeds to land, farm-mortgages, bank credits, consols, shares and bonds. (Consols, shares, and bonds, represent sub-divided proportions of the battle-booty.) He also climbs to success over his prostrate rivals—for there is no other road. Success and money come to him *only*, when he has outwitted his rivals, and finally triumphed in the ruthless rough-and-tumble of daily, hourly conflict. The "Business Man" is a conquerer of the most merciless, stony-hearted, and cruel kind; but we must not blame him for that. If he displays a particle of human sympathy, with the multitudinous victims of his business methods, he is immediately out-generaled, bankrupted, ruined by his rivals, with more iron in their strategy—more hardiness in their hearts. A kind-hearted man is always a failure in "business," and he is always a failure in "war." War means thorough-going smashing-up of your opponent, so that he may be prevented from smashing you up; and it is "ditto, ditto, ditto," in all the parallel phases of Commerce and Trade.

With "money in his purse" the successful businessman is able to support a family, and rear up his children in an environment of comparative freedom, and women are sharp to perceive this. In such matters the female mind is preternaturally acute. Except in sexual matters a woman has no more brains than a cock-sparrow—but in questions of marriage and love, she is an expert. Other things being equal, women prefer a rich-man to a poor-man for a husband—and they are scientifically justified. He who is without wealth amidst unlimited quantities of it, is either a coward, a born slave or a lunatic; and no self-respecting woman should marry such an imbecile.

The resolute and brave, never 'hunger' to the grave.

The gallant and the bold, never lack for—gold.

With the possession of an "independence," a man is freed to materialize his ideals; and if he is "well born" it is impossible for his ideals to partake of the ignoble.

Gold is a fierce resolvent. It is the sublimated extract of Victory. It is the property—the booty—of the Strong. "Whoever has sixpence," writes Carlyle, "is sovereign over all men to the extent of that sixpence; commands cooks to feed him, philosophers to teach him, *kings to mount guard over him*—to the extent of that sixpence." Therefore all men who would obtain freedom must obtain wealth 'by hook or by crook,' or as R.L. Stevenson rhymes it: "You also scan your life horizon, for all that you can clap your eyes on." To become a child-bearer of a mere hireling, a day drudge, is the last resort of a sensible female.

Dowerless women never regard a poor lover with enthusiastic favour: except in conventional romances. Without being capable of logical reasoning, yet women intuitively comprehend that "there is oft a lack of courage in the race of bondmen." If a man possesses wealth (no matter how obtained) he can pick and choose among the most delightful darlings in the land: nay, he can buy them (if he wants to)—by the carload. Behind all the hypocritic veneer of piety and fashion, women of all ranks are still a marketable commodity. Whenever the supply exceeds the demand, they are straightway transmuted into magdelenes, concubines, slaves (or "new women"). When few in number (as in young colonies) they possess a certain proportion of selective influence, but when for every eligible man, there is a score of eligible women, their market value dwindles, and instead of 'selecting,' they become the 'selected' or as Darwin puts it: "The sexual struggle is of two kinds. In the one it is between the individuals of the same sex, generally the males, in order to drive away or kill their rivals, the females remaining passive; while in the other, the struggle is likewise between the individuals of the same sex, generally the females, which no longer remain passive, but select the more agreeable partners." (Vide *Descent of Man*)

In a reasonably natural Society, the most vigorous males would possess Property and Power. Consequently (in accordance with the instincts of sex-attraction), they would also obtain possession and impregnate, the best and handsomest feminines, leaving the ovum-bearing residue to be fertilized by the less vigorous males.

144

In an unnatural system of Society (such as the fiendish socialistic scheme, amidst which we now retrograde) weaklings, dotards, and semi-madmen are deliberately permitted to retain Property-Privileges; that they are manifestly unable to defend *if put to the test.* The 'Law' defends the Unfit. Consequently opulent weaklings preponderate in the selection and retention of the finest females. Resultantly the children of such unnatural unions seldom reach even average perfection. More often than otherwise they are a shame and a malison to their kindrid. "The sons of vicious and very corrupt men," wrote Plutarch ages ago, "reproduce the very nature of their parents."

This nation literally swarms with vile semi-idiotic mannikins (leprous wretches, damned in the womb) whose presence among us, is a standing menace to all things truly Great and Noble. It is not by breeding meeklings and stunted profligates, that nobility of national character is evolved. Why should diseased and ignoble animals (rich or poor) be encouraged to populate luxurious wigwams, with fragile, anemic, bottle-fed, scrofulous dwarfs; when nature demands their wholesale segregation—by the edge of the sword?

Dr. Haycraft suggests that Society should socialistically segregate the Unfit, but that is manifestly out of the question, inasmuch as Society is incompetant to provide a testing standard, sufficiently absolute and accurate, to decide satisfactorily who are and who are not the "Unfit." Nature however has provided that standard, and it is *unending conflict* between rival interests: with women, power, and property as the contestant's final prize. The surest, fairest, and most scientific method of redistributing monopolized plunder and accumulated privilege is—unlimited struggle.

Let the Best Men win! Is that not the Logic of events of Science, of Fact and of Nature?

Why should Anglo-Saxondom doltishly stand guard over the copulations of opulent decadents, and shoals of creeping unwarlike proletarians? "Nor is anyone so careless (writes Charles Darwin) as to breed from his worst animals. Even savages, when compelled from extreme want, to kill some of their animals, *would destroy the worst and preserve the best.*"

The Fit are not the individuals who merely inherit stolen property; or obtain peaceful possession thereof by subterraneanism; but those who deliberately, and openly proprietorise themselves. If taboos were not so insanely reverenced, proprietors who are incapables would be unceremoniously pushed aside (most probably) to make room for *better men.*

If those 'in possession' victoriously prove their capacity, then their prerogatives cannot be abrogated or abridged; but should they fail, then their vanquishers—presumably better men—are biologically justified in disposing of them. "Let the best man win" is an assertive, at once popular, scientific, and suggestive. The mastership of the Ablest Man is exactly what science and circumstances demand. In Nature an organism's right is commensurate with its mentality and physique. In the realm of Cosmic Law, the only Statute of Limitations is superior Power.

A-priori "rights" are as non-existent as the gods and ghosts, and moral taboos of the pontiffs and pastors. Therefore the police-officer's club (being in harmony with the dynamic necessities of matter and motion) is part and parcel of the Divine Order. So are clubs in general. Men shall ring around each other, in a fierce unending strife; each shall strive to 'beat' his brother, wile for wile, and life for life.

If legislative injunctions, and other bogey contrivances were wholly disregarded, then the Strongest and the Boldest (therefore the Wisest) would by fertilizing their pick of the best damsels per marriage, transmit their own right-royal qualities to their immediate descendants. Upon similar principles second-rate males would of necessity pair-off with second-rate females. This by cumulative atavism, and interbreeding of underlings, would gradually tend to eliminate, subjugate, and efface the seed of the servile-minded—the superstitious and the over intellectualized.

Heredity virtues can only be maintained, by keeping them in constant use. Hence the biological necessity of unmerciful struggles between individuals and groups of individuals. As with muscles and organs of the body, so human aptitudes are developed by use and attenuated by non-use. Nearly all the masterful qualities, mental and physical, that have ever distinguished the elite of mankind, have originated in conflict.

Racial rottenness (the conjoint result of holy hydrophobia and State-regulated hybridism) can only be eliminated by an intelligent application to the breeding of human beings—of the principles of natural selection, conjoined with conscious rejection, culminating from time to time in deadly conflicts. War is the most important phase of racial, sex and tribal evolution.

One panic-stricken coward may cause the loss of a battle—and the loss of one battle may decide for ages (perhaps forever), the fate of a Race. Hence the necessity of breeding men who are fighters—fighters in their heart. Hence also the need of training them, from boyhood up, to conquer and overthrow their oppressors and personal enemies—at any cost—at any peril. By no known alchemy can a race of warriors and freemen be evoluted out of a "flock of bleating, baaing, lapping lambs, suckled on teats of priest-rid dams."

"The qualities which have enabled the Teutonic races to play their wonderful part in the history of Europe, are well displayed in the valiant sons of Tancred, of Hautonville—William Iron Arm— Robert Guiscard—themselves in Apulia and Sicily. They were a vigorous race, large of limb, stout of heart, tenacious of will; with abundant physical energy, taking their pleasures in drinking and hunting. They had broad shoulders, fair hair, blue eyes; as we see in Anna Comnenia's portrait of the son of Robert Guiscard, Bohemnd, Prince of Tarentum, who was 'a cubit taller than the tallest man...with blue eyes, his cheeks tinted with golden red." (Taylor's Origin Aryan Race.)

🦅 9 🦅

All hireling labor is corroding, corrupting, degrading, devilish. Cursed is the brow that sweats—for hire, and the back that bends to a master's burden. Calloused hands imply calloused minds. "Virtue in bondage," what an insane paradox?

There is something mutilated about men who exert the strength of their body or mind, for the enrichment of Taskmasters, and women are not slow to perceive it. Women are never deluded with the maniac philosophy that "Jack is as good as his master." Indian squaws have no admiration for the "brave" who has never taken a scalp; and white women have even less for the 'bearded man,' who—amidst gold and silver by the ton—lives from hand to mouth, like a mangy cur.

The bolder and more aggressive men are, the more women of all classes admire them—and vice verse. Thus the surging ebb and flow of attraction and of gravitation is ever directed toward—the impregnation of the Fair—by the Strong. How glorious beneath the sun is the union of the Beautiful and the Brave.

Soiled hands (if soiled for market hire or the payment of tribute) imply a soiled manhood—a biological organism of 'low degree.' Labor performed for oneself is passible—when performed for others, it is utterly debasing—ruinous to brain and body.

From the beginning of time, the defeated classes have ever been the laboring classes—the tenants—the vassals—the sans-cullotes: and the conquerors (their heirs or assigns) have always provided (or hired) the priests, generals, taskmasters, and rulers. This is as true of the United States (a European colony) as it was of Thebes, Troy, Babylon, Persia, Carthage, Rome.

"Fallen from primeval innocence and ease,
(When thornless fields employed him, but to please)
The laborer toils—and from his dripping brow
Moistens the lengthening furrows of the plough.
In vain he scorns and spurns his altered state,
Tries each poor shift, and strives to cheat his fate;
In vain new-shapes his name; to shun the ill—
Serf, hireling, help—the curse pursues him still;
Changeless the doom remains: the mincing phrase,
May mock high-heaven, but not reverse its ways."*

The only apparent difference, between the bondservant of antiquity, and the "educated" hireling of to-day, is—the thorough-going lunacy of the latter. The ancient Servi *knew* that they were held in bondage by force of arms; but modern slaves being born, maniacal degenerates, don't know it. Indeed the free workmen of England and America, can be compared to nothing more appropriate than Ibsens "hero," who fancied himself a reigning monarch (with the fate of empires in his nod) when inside a Cairo madhouse his head was ceremoniously encircled with a diadem of straw. ("His brow is wet with *honest* sweat," is the National Anthem of an insane asylum.)

From whatever side we view him, the average hireling is a shameless, contemptible being. He cannot be classified among "men," any more than a capon can be classified as a gamecock. Continuous drudgery stiffens his body—ossifies both his hand and brain—makes him an idiot in fact. Even women (indulgent though they be) regard him as a disdainful object, incapable of either great thoughts, great deeds, or of providing them with a home. Hirelings are nearly always on the verge of pauperdom—always praying, howling, and weeping before their *Taskmasters,* crying out with a loud voice like spoilt babies, "O don't hurt us—don't hurt us—we are so 'good'—so law-abiding—we love Jesus so!" Capitalists, kings, and presidents never take these servile hounds into consideration—*nor do sensible women.* In grand affairs hirelings are merely inventoried as so much raw material or so many head of cattle; and in sexual affairs, they must of necessity, mate themselves with second-rate women—who cannot possibly find anything more to their taste.

What woman in her senses desires to be a breeder of drudges, lunatics, and sans-cullotes?

---

* "The Hireling and the Slave,"—W.J. Grayson, 1856.

The very idea of "Labor" is in chains and yokes. There is no dignity in a bent back—no glory in a perspiring brow—no honor in greasy copper-riveted rags. There is nothing very delectable in picks, shovels, and calloused paws. 'Dignity of Labor!'—Dignity of hell!

What is *grand* in a horny hand?

What is *free* in a bended knee?

What is *brave* in a pauper grave?

What is *bold* in a lack of gold?

O ye generations of Christ-deluded imbeciles! Ye swarms of moonstruck meeklings! Ye burnt out cinders of men!—ye blessing lambs! One day! One day! ye shall be flung to the lions! Behold! I spit upon your Idols—your Opinions. Now would I pour molten hell through the ventricles of your soul.

"O wretched minds of men! O blind hearts! not to see in what darkness of life, and in what dangers, is spent this little term of human existence. For as children are frightened at fancied objects in the gloom, so we in broad daylight, often fear what deserves no more to be feared, than the shadows the children dread in the dark, and fancy they must exist."

END OF BOOK ONE

P.S. Book II will be issued when circumstances demand it.

7

THE LOGIC OF TO-DAY

Inferior organisms succumb and perish or are enslaved.
Superior organisms survive, propagate and POSSESS.
—Darwin.

'All men are created equal' —is an infernal Lie.

Not by speechifying and majority votes can the great
questions of To-Day be settled . . . by iron and by blood.
—Bismarck

****

Might was Right when Ceasar bled
                        upon the stones of Rome,
Might was Right when Joshua led
                        his hordes o'er Jordan's foam,
And Might was Right when German troops
                        poured down through Paris gay;
It's the Gospel of the Ancient World
                        and the Logic of To-Day.

Behind all Kings and Presidents—
                        all Government and Law,
Are army-corps and cannoneers—
                        to hold the world in awe.
And sword-strong races own the earth
                        and ride the Conqueror's Car—
And *Liberty* has ne'er been won,
                        except by deeds of war.

150

What are the lords of hoarded gold—
                    the silent *Semite* rings?
What are the plunder-patriots—
                    high-pontiffs, priests and kings?
What are they but bold master-minds,
                    best fitted for the fray
Who comprehend and vanquish by—
                    the Logic of To-Day.

Cain's knotted club is scepter still—
                    the "Rights of Man" is fraud:
Christ's Ethics are for creeping things—
                    true manhood smiles at "God."
For Might is Right when empires sink
                    in storms of steel and flame;
And it is *right* when weakling breeds—
                    are hunted down like game.

Then what's the use of dreaming dreams—
                    that "each shall get his own"
By forceless votes of meek-eyed thralls,
                    who blindly sweat and moan?
No! a curse is on their cankered brains—
                    their very bones decay:
Go! trace your fate in the Iron Game,
                    is the Logic of To-Day.

The Strong must ever rule the Weak,
                    is grim Primordial Law—
On earth's broad racial threshing floor,
                    the Meek are beaten straw—
Then ride to Power o'er foemen's necks
                    let *nothing* bar your way:
If you are *fit* you'll rule and reign,
                    is the Logic of To-Day.

You must prove your Right by deeds of Might—
                    of splendor and renown.
If need-be march through flames of hell,
                    to dash opponents down—
If need-be die on scaffold high—
                    in the morning's misty grey:
For *"Liberty or Death"* is still
                    the Logic of To-Day.

151

Might was Right when Gideon led,
                         the "chosen" tribes of old,
And it was right when Titus burnt,
                         their Temple roofed with gold:
And Might was Right from Bunker's Hill,
                         to far Manilla Bay,
By land and flood it's wrote in blood—
                         the Gospel of To-Day.

"Put not your trust in princes"
                         is a saying old and true,
"Put not your hope in Governments"
                         translateth it anew.
All 'Books of Law' and 'Golden Rules'
                         are fashioned to betray:
'The Survival of the Strongest'
                         is the Gospel of To-Day.

Might was Right when Carthage flames
                         lit up the Punic foam—
And—when the naked steel of Gaul
                         weighed down the spoil of Rome;
And Might was Right when Richmond fell—
                         and at Thermopylae—
It's the Logic of the Ancient World—
                         and the Gospel of To-Day.

Where pendant suns in millions swing,
                         around this whirling earth,
It's Might, it's Force that holds the brakes,
                         and steers through life and death:
Force governs all organic life,
                         inspires all Right and Wrong.
It's nature's plan to weed-out man,
                         and *test* who are the Strong.

THE HIGHER LAW

From Sandy Hook to London tower
From Jaffa to Japan,
They can take who have the power
They may keep who can.

The law of Heaven and Hell
Stupendous and divine
The highest, holiest law of all
That governs "mine and thine."

The law it is of Sun and Star,
Of President and Pope—
It is "the prisoner at the bar"
The gallows and the rope.

It is the lawyer and his fee;
The shearer and his sheep—
The eagle soaring swift and free;
The Dreadnaught on the deep.

It is the Bond; it is the Loan—
The profit and the loss—
The usurer on his Bullion Throne—
The Idol of the Cross.

It is the Goth; it is the Hun—
The tyrant and his prey,
And flame and saber, club and gun;
O, taxes that we pay!

It is the law of all the climes,
And all the things to be;
And all the bold tremendous times
That you and I shall see.

From Sandy Hook to London tower,
From Greenland to Japan—
They will take who have the Power
And they may keep who can.

Redbeards Review

153

PAX VOBISCUM

Fill high your vaults with booty,
  Bid evolution cease,
And chant Belzchazzar's anthem:
  "O, Baal preserve the peace."

YOU WILL ALSO WANT TO READ:

☐ **THE MYTH OF NATURAL RIGHTS, by L.A. Rollins.** Does your "right to life" protect you from an assailant's bullets? Does your "right to privacy" keep government agencies from snooping through your mail? NO! Rights are only *imaginary* shields, yet since the days of Thomas Jefferson, Americans have been indoctrinated to believe they have these "natural" rights, which are ignored by governments and other coercers whenever inconvenient. This book dissects all the major arguments for natural rights, cutting through the faulty logic to the underlying dogma. Eye-opening reading for those who find that no one respects those "rights" they think they're entitled to. *5½ x 8½, 50 pp, bibliography, soft cover.* **$4.95 (Order Number 94067)**

☐ **THE RIGHT TO BE GREEDY, For Ourselves.** An underground Situationist classic for years, this thought-provoking book is finally back in print! This is a *communist* defense of greed and selfishness. It proposes that egoism is the highest form of communism, that all morality is a form of self-sacrifice, and that the true egoist transcends petty materialism for a more rewarding form of self-fulfillment. One of the most challenging books you will ever read! *5½ x 8½, 94 pp, soft cover.* **$5.95 (Order Number 94062)**

☐ **NATIVE AMERICAN ANARCHISM, by Eunice M. Schuster.** James J. Martin called this, "The only work of merit by an American on native anarchism." Miss Schuster traces the rise and fall of this country's most notorious political movement, including new-age anti-authoritarian communities, the labor movement, the struggle for sexual freedom, and more. A painstakingly documented, well-written history. *5½ x 8½, 202 pp, indexed, bibliography, soft cover.* **$9.95 (Order Number 94068)**

And Much More! We offer the very finest in controversial and unusual books — please turn to the catalog announcement on the next page.

CONTROVERSIAL AND UNUSUAL BOOKS!!!

"Yes, there are books about the skills of apocalypse -- spying, surveillance, fraud, wire-tapping, smuggling, self-defense, lockpicking, gunmanship, eavesdropping, car chasing, civil warfare, surviving jail, and dropping out of sight. Apparently writing books is the way mercenaries bring in spare cash between wars. The books are useful, and it's good the information is freely available (and they definitely inspire interesting dreams), but their advice should be taken with a salt shaker or two and all your wits. A few of these volumes are truly scary. Loompanics is the best of the Libertarian suppliers who carry them. Though full of 'you'll-wish-you'd-read-these-when-it's-too-late' rhetoric, their catalog is genuinely informative."
-THE NEXT WHOLE EARTH CATALOG

Now available:
THE BEST BOOK CATALOG IN THE WORLD!!!

- *Large 8½ x 11 size!*
- *More than 500 of the most controversial and unusual books ever printed!!!*
- *YOU can order EVERY book listed!!!*
- *Periodic Supplements to keep you posted on the LATEST titles available!!!*

We offer hard-to-find books on the world's most unusual subjects. Here are a few of the topics covered IN DEPTH in our exciting new catalog:

- *Hiding/concealment of physical objects! A complete section of the best books ever written on hiding things!*
- *Fake ID/Alternate Identities! The most comprehensive selection of books on this little-known subject ever offered for sale! You have to see it to believe it!*
- *Investigative/Undercover methods and techniques! Professional secrets known only to a few, now revealed for YOU to use! Actual police manuals on shadowing and surveillance!*
- *And much, much more, including Locks and Locksmithing, Self Defense, Intelligence Increase, Life Extension, Money-Making Opportunities, and much, much more!*

Our book catalog is truly THE BEST BOOK CATALOG IN THE WORLD! Order yours today -- you will be very pleased, we know.

(Our catalog is free with the order of any book on the previous page -- or is $2.00 if ordered by itself.)

Loompanics Unlimited
PO Box 1197
Pt Townsend, WA 98368
USA